Dear Sister

A Letter to the Sisterhood

MEGAN WOODING

MWS Publishing
Wallingford, CT

ISBN-13: 978-0-578-59743-0

Published by MWS Publishing
Wallingford, CT

Printed in the United States of America
First Edition 2019

Design: Make Your Mark Publishing Solutions
Editing: Make Your Mark Publishing Solutions

Contents

Dedication

This book is dedicated to my nieces, Eowyn, Ruby,
Emersyn, Storia, and their generation of women.
May you always know your full worth.
May you know how to choose yourselves.
May we create the sisterhood you need to
become the women you are meant to be.

Introduction

This book is an apology to all the women I missed out on when I was afraid that connection would make me weak. It's a thank you to women who have been guiding forces in my life and to those who are already sisters in arms. It's an invitation to connection and personal reclamation. This book isn't exclusive to women who practice and claim faith; however, I do discuss my experiences and beliefs from growing up female in the evangelical Christian church.

Christianity is not only a religion, it is also a powerful social construct. It has been a catalyst for both great good and great evil. Thanks to colonizing countries using forms of Christianity as tools of subjugation and conquest, most of us have some personal history with Christian faith whether we identify as Christian or not. I didn't write this book to present tidy answers or formulas. I wrote this book to ask big, juicy questions. I don't expect you to agree with everything (or maybe even anything) I've written here. I do hope this book makes you look at things from new perspectives and start conversations. Where you take them is up to you.

In January of 2018, I had the privilege of attending a workshop led by one of my favorite authors, Erin Brown. At the end, she had all of us stand in two circles and repeat affirmations to each other. First, the outer circle to the inner circle then vice versa. When the affirmation was complete, one circle shifted, and we met new partners. I came face to face with woman after woman, repeating back and forth with her words of encouragement and apology. Many of these women I had never met, yet their faces mirrored the very things I felt in my deepest soul about being seen and valued, about my needs and my wounds. Every affirmation started with the words *Dear Sister* and they were the words echoing in my heart as I left.

After the sister circle, Erin quipped that if this was what church felt like, she would be there all the time. I knew one thing for sure—I felt more profound love, grace, genuine confession, and repentance that night than I have in most church services I have attended through many years of organized religion. My takeaway was a little different, though. I thought back to all the women I have met and talked to in the church struggling to meet God through a haze of religious expectations and practices passed down for millennia. What words did I have for them? What solace? What sisterhood?

And so, *Dear Sister* was born. A letter to my sisters. An invitation to community and healing. An exploration of a God who made every one of us exactly as God meant to and does not punish us for our humanity, our limits, or our needs. An examination of how we have allowed our culture of hustling and consumerism to contaminate our most sacred spaces. A rally cry to build safe and brave community together.

Thank you for journeying with me.

Apologies & Affirmations

Dear sister, I apologize for not seeing you. I couldn't see past my own fears. I see you now, *all* of you. I hold space for your vulnerabilities and traumas. I support your creativity and magic.

Dear sister, I apologize for not saying "me too" sooner. Your experience matters. Your wounds matter. I hold brave space for you and your healing.

Dear sister, I apologize for the shushing and silencing you have experienced in the name of faith and religion. Your story, your voice, and your energy are so needed. I am ready to listen.

Dear sister, you owe no one any part of you. Your gifts are yours to share on your terms within your boundaries. This is not selfish; it is healing and honoring of your humanity and limits.

Dear sister, I apologize for judging your holiness, your spirituality, your commitment based on how you choose to show up in your faith. Your worth, validity, presence, and beliefs are not determined by how you choose to serve and be seen.

Dear sister, I apologize for the shame you have been handed in the name of faith and religion. You don't have to keep it; it is not holy. Nothing about you is shameful, not your body, not your desires, not your need for rest.

Dear sister, I am sorry the church has not always been a safe space for you to heal from the trauma you have experienced. We can create that space now. You are heard now. I believe you.

Dear sister, I need your leadership and voice in my life. Your story matters. Together, we are unstoppable.

Dear sister, I apologize for building walls instead of bridges. I was afraid of more hurt, more judgement. Now I know we are stronger, brighter, and more grounded together.

-Inspired by the Sister Circle activity led by Erin Brown during her Sovereign workshop-

1

Finding Worthiness

Dear Sister,

The foundation of all our beliefs in life is what we believe about ourselves. What we believe about ourselves shapes what we believe about other people and, dangerously often, what those of us who participate in faith traditions believe about our God. So first, I'm going to share how I came to claim and believe in my own personal worthiness.

When I believed harmful things about myself—I was lazy, didn't finish anything, was okay at things but never good enough to be noticed or listened to—it didn't matter how many people told me otherwise. All it took was one voice confirming that story I told myself every day to cement it as my truth. Maybe most dangerous was my belief that if people knew the real me, they would abandon me. This kept me constantly hustling for the approval of others and sculpting myself to their opinions of me.

For a long time, my idea of success was just to feel okay. To not feel constantly unseen, overwhelmed, and unworthy. I craved emotional stability. Only recently have I learned there is so much wonder past learning to surf the waves of my emotions. There is purpose, there is community, and there is the most wonderful and inspiring work.

But to get to those things, we must do *this* work. We must first understand where we find our worthiness and why. Only then can we detach enough from our core belief systems to gently sift through them and consider if they are really serving us and what light our chosen faith may shed on them. I am profoundly grateful that you are on this journey with me.

All my love,
Megan

I grew up in conservative, evangelical Christian communities. There's a sliding scale of lifestyle choices associated with conservative faith. If you want to place me, I was allowed to wear pants in the form of snow pants; otherwise, I was always in skirts and dresses. I didn't watch TV (except for important occasions like elections and sometimes football games) or listen to popular music. My family fast forwarded through the more "sexual" parts of Bing Crosby's *White Christmas*, but we watched it. Oh, and I was homeschooled. We were friends with others on either side of us along the spectrum, those who were even more conservative than we were and those who took more liberties and listened to music with a "back beat" (also known as music with drums) and wore jeans.

As a kid, I was asked if I was Amish a lot. I've always been a literal person, so it took several times before I realized the other child asking was not looking for an explanation of the theological and lifestyle differences between my family and Amish communities. They meant I was different, I was weird, and the closest association other kids had to someone like me was the stereotypical mental image they had of the Amish. I'm at a place now where I can look back at childhood pictures and see a cute kid in French braids and clothes lovingly hand sewn by my mom, but at the time, dressing like I'd come out of *Little House on the Prairie* had social drawbacks.

Their questions always started with why I dressed how I did, moved on to see if we shared any common knowledge of TV shows (we didn't), music (still no), or popular toys ... When the interrogation proved we shared absolutely nothing in common, the question dropped: "What, are you Amish or something?" Apparently, ten-year-olds from the year 2000 thought "Amish" meant not watching TV or listening to popular music, wearing long dresses, and going to church. When I protested that we used electricity, wore patterned clothes, and didn't wear head coverings, markers of actual Amish communities, they didn't seem convinced.

It's very possible the kids I met as a seven-to-eleven-year-old were just confused and blunt. Some of them seemed genuinely curious. Others found that "different" could be weaponized. One of the few activities I participated in with non-homeschooled kids was week-long summer camps at our local living history museum. I loved these, partially because *everyone* wore a traditional costume for the week. It leveled the playing field, although it still didn't take kids long to figure out I wasn't anything like them. One year, an older girl (probably all of twelve) decided I was an easy target. She would be nice to my face then make fun of me when she thought I wasn't watching. I caught her in the act by the end of the week, and she was thoroughly embarrassed. I enjoyed that for ten minutes, but the shame of the experience stuck with me. There are so many forms and degrees of bullying. No one physically beat me up or wrote hateful letters. I don't want to diminish the experiences of those who have dealt with oppressive bullies daily for years, but this was a form of bullying for me. Maybe, like in the case of the older girl from summer camp, it was intentional, but even the unintended interrogations fed my internal critic. They confirmed that I couldn't belong.

Anyone who has experienced bullying as a child or adult knows the sting of shame for being somehow different, for being other, for being intrinsically *wrong* for being who we are. A bully's message is always the same—that we are shameful and unworthy.

I feel like saying I grew up in church minimizes the impact religion had on my childhood. My family was all in. We read the Bible every morning before Dad left for work (usually). At the end of the day, we gathered for praise time. My mom created day-long programs with scriptures, hymns, and readings for the major holidays, and I'm barely scratching the surface. We also went to church.

A favorite verse of my evangelical childhood pastors was, "The heart is deceitful above all things, and desperately wicked; who can know it?" (Jeremiah 17:9, NKJV). The constant focus on the depravity of humanity, of myself, taught me that I am, above all things, deceitful and desperately wicked. Once again, who I was as a human was wrong. This time, there wasn't an easy explanation of cultural differences. This time, it was just me. My pastors and childhood bullies both fed the worst bully— the one in my head.

As an adult, I call shaming someone through religion spiritual bullying. I'm sure this wasn't the intention of any of my childhood pastors. They believed fully in what they were doing. In my life, however, their impact has outweighed their intentions. Their constant focus on my depravity as a fallen human taught me I couldn't trust myself. The expectation that I adhere to a specific image of Christian femininity to belong was just another reminder that I never could. Believing my heart to be "deceitful and wicked" taught me if I really wanted something, it was probably bad for me. It taught me to never prioritize my needs or wants. It silenced my voice. I was valuable only for my service. I was valuable for my "ministry smile." I was valuable because of the things I did, not because of who I was or who I was created to be.

The example adults set in my church communities carried out this theme, too. They hustled and served, and when they were tired, just said they needed more of Jesus. Especially the women. There was no celebration of autonomy or respect for personal boundaries. We would tell you our worth was based in faith, but our lives showed our worth was based in our accomplishments. When worth is based in performance, it's like mailing a handwritten personal invitation to Perfectionism to move in.

It took me years of study, growth, and therapy to celebrate my identity and gifts. By the time I started claiming my own identity in faith, I had been practicing perfectionism for years.

Scientific studies have proven that the more we repeat thoughts and actions, the more efficiently our brains process them. This is how we learn new skills, how we learn sports, movement, musical instruments. The same goes for the thought patterns we repeat constantly like, "What if I'm not good enough?" "They didn't mean that compliment," "I can't reach that goal," "They don't really love me." These thoughts we repeat regularly become our default thought patterns. They feel so automatic that we don't even question them. We accept them as part of who we are.

Kids taught me I didn't belong. Pastors taught me not only that I didn't belong, but God thought I was unworthy of belonging. Pastors and other faith teachers taught me I wasn't trustworthy. They taught me my worth came from my performance in faith and life. They taught me to look for Jesus in specific places and prescribed ways. They taught me the harder my life and faith felt, the holier I was. They taught me I had to bury my agency and autonomy to be accepted by my God. This was their version of all the "S" words that make me wince now—submission, sacrifice, and service. Above all, they taught me that their acceptance was conditional. When we accept unworthiness as our truth, we become our own bullies, and there is no easy escape.

My internal critic was well fed. As I searched for ways to cope with the shame of my unworthiness, Perfectionism came to my rescue.

I recently sat and talked about the family history of perfectionism with my mom. This is her perspective:

I confused striving for excellence with striving for perfection. Because of that, I put a burden on myself and our family that I didn't even know was there. We are thirty years into a handyman special of a house that is still not finished. I have had to accept a lot less than perfection in my home, and that hasn't been easy for me. Perfectionism has been a real curse. It has sneaky ways of coming back into our lives.

I thought if I had higher standards for myself than anyone else could have for me, I would be able to avoid their disappointment and rejection. As a baby empath, the only way I could feel stable was to make sure everyone around me was always happy. I thought if I figured everyone out and stayed ten steps ahead of them, I could control not only their emotions, but how they viewed me. This was as exhausting as it sounds.

The only way I could feel safe was to be in control.

My sense of identity was crafted out of achieving specific roles in my life perfectly. I had to be the perfect wife, the perfect employee, the perfect Christian.

I spent my childhood, adolescence, and early adulthood practicing perfectionism. As I grew, so did the roles and expectations I had for myself. The problem is, from all I can tell, life wasn't meant to be lived perfectly. Life isn't meant to be completely controlled. Life expands, grows, and overwhelms us, and this is what makes it beautiful. After it's devastating, it's beautiful.

My precarious tower of perfectly balanced roles toppled in 2014. My husband, Chris, lost his job, and I began to have increased responsibilities at my own job that I could not physically stay on top of. I found myself crying in the bathroom at work, which I hadn't done since I worked my first Christmas season in retail. I was also spending a minimum of twenty minutes every morning lying in bed convincing myself that, yes, I needed to go to work because I really liked my house and wanted to keep living in it. There's nothing like showing up to work ten to twenty minutes late and feeling like you've just fought the biggest battle of your day.

Perfectionism often comes with friends, and mine was best friends with the depression monster. Depression followed me from my teens in New York to my adult, married life in Connecticut. I experience depression in an emotional cocktail of numbness, apathy, and overwhelm. I finally figured out I needed some new coping skills because my plan to just control all things was not working. I remember reading a Humans of New York post about a man who became a dog walker, and it was exactly what he wanted to be doing. I was so jealous of this guy because he seemed so happy and fulfilled. I just wanted to hide from the world. I finally went to therapy instead.

I'm not exactly sure what I expected therapy to be like. Mystical maybe? I definitely wanted it to be transactional. I wanted to trade my problems and money for custom coping skills to carry me through my work days with a sense of euphoric calm. Instead, my therapist told me things like, "You need to develop internal boundaries." I wrote in my journal afterwards, *No sh*t, Sherlock. That's why I'm here. How do I get the internal boundaries?* I didn't even have external boundaries. As we progressed, though, I painstakingly began the process of getting to know myself then intentionally teaching the people I loved and who loved me what I needed to feel safe and whole.

My friend Heather and I compared notes on our experiences of therapy, and she said:

> *I didn't go to therapy until my husband, Joe, encouraged me to go. I thought therapy was bad and sinful. The first therapist I had was awful, but I didn't know it. When I moved to Maine, I realized I could pick, and I found one I loved. She fixed a lot for me, and although I'm still pretty broken, I graduated therapy. She showed me how to fix things myself instead of just listening to me talk.*

*She helped me cope a lot. Therapy was rough. I would
have to not do anything else on a therapy day. Now, I
miss it. I still read a lot, but now I know how to stop a
thinking error and fix it.*

The biggest goal I had in therapy was developing
groundedness and resilience. I wanted to know that I could
handle whatever came at me. I didn't expect life to be easy or
struggle free, but I wanted to be able to take it in stride. I asked
my therapist if she thought this was doable. Do people really live
like this? Everyone I knew was also regularly overwhelmed and
exhausted, and we all just thought that was life. She told me that,
yes, she thought it was possible, but it would take work, and she
couldn't say how that would present in my life. Perfectionism
heard, "I can earn this" and was in.

It took years for me to realize, in my bones, that it really,
really isn't about earning. The effort and motivation I put
into my personal development did, however, pay off. At the
suggestion of my therapist, I started actively prioritizing what
I wanted. This might seem weird for anyone who hasn't heard
that JOY is an acronym for "Jesus then others then you," but I
prioritized almost everything else over what I really wanted in
life. "Want" was a dangerous word full of feelings and devoid of
logic. "Want" was one of the creepy kids under the robe of The
Ghost of Christmas Present in George C. Scott's *A Christmas
Carol*. If anything, the things I *wanted* were suspect. It felt safer
to prioritize everything else. I prioritized Chris, I prioritized
work, I prioritized convenience. I prioritized the other things in
my life I felt I needed to be okay, when what I really needed to
be okay was to get to know who I was and prioritize her.

"What do I really want?" became a mantra. I had found so
much of my own worthiness in faith, getting to know myself
through compassion. Religious folks seem to love the "more of
Jesus, less of self" mantra. I react to this strongly, not because I

9

don't want more of Jesus, but because it ignores that in Christian faith tradition, self was created carefully and lovingly in the image of our Creator. Less of ego? Sure. Less shame? I'm in. But less self? I need to uncover my *whole* created self to fully live into who I was made to be.

The first time (and, okay, many subsequent times) I heard Nichole Nordeman's song "Dear Me," I started crying. It hit me so hard that I was made exactly as I was meant to be. God didn't mess up the parts of me that I always chafed against or tried to hide in efforts to appear more worthy. I wasn't made to love too fiercely. I wasn't made to be graceful or extroverted. I had stopped growing at 5'2" on purpose and didn't get the thick, luscious hair I had pined for as a kid. I was created a woman with all the challenges, disadvantages, and pain that comes with it because this is how I can best love others well. I was created to need a full eight hours of sleep a night to remotely function and was given a finely tuned sense of justice and a drive to see equity achieved.

It hurts to feel limited. It hurts to feel powerless. But as Alice Walker says, "The biggest way people give up their power is by not believing they have any." Let me rephrase that: The biggest way we Christians give up our power in faith is by not believing, understanding, and embodying the reality that we have not been given the spirit of fear but of love, power and—my favorite—*a sound mind* (2 Tim 1:7, NKJV).

God making me exactly as God meant to, in Imago Dei, means my heart has good desires. That taking care of my body, my mind, and my soul is honoring divine gifts. That my intuition as a woman, which gets a bad rap, is a way I can connect deeply in faith. When we start actually believing that God made us in Imago Dei, the door to understanding our worthiness swings open.

No matter how harsh fundamentalist teachings were, from the time I was a child, I knew down to my toes that God knew everything about me already. We couldn't be disconnected no matter how "desperately wicked" my heart was. Through all the misunderstanding and loneliness, I felt God was the only one who knew it all. As I began sifting through my worthiness, I had many questions like, "Why did You create me this way?" "Are these feelings, desires, needs from You, or are they just mine?" "If they are just mine, are they inherently wrong?"

My friend Kelly recently shared her worthiness journey with me:

I had a huge identity crisis for most of my life. I didn't know where I belonged. I was abandoned as a child. I was a teenage runaway and a drug addict. You can do the math and think about all the things that can happen to somebody during that time. I didn't know who I was, even for me. I'm grateful that I had that faith journey. I'm grateful it put me on this path. But I also got to a point where I was exhausted, trying to prove my worthiness in the church. In some church circles, fitting in is more important than understanding why you're there.

Worthiness is a new concept for me. It's something I've stepped into in the last year, really fully understanding my worth, not to other people but to myself. I've spent my whole life trying to prove myself, trying to fit in, feeling like I was at a disadvantage because of how I grew up and not having a lot of the opportunities other people have. Understanding my worthiness to be enough for me and not mattering to anyone else is a huge switch for me.

Although I always felt affirmed relationally in faith, I had a lot to unpack and discover about my identity. Theological discussion can sound like people are telling me things that just sound wrong about a trusted friend. After a while, I started wondering if I'm the one who doesn't know them. Only as I delved into searching for peace and real security did I realize how much old teachings undermined my life and faith.

Separating church and state is important in a governmental capacity, but even there, we see religious beliefs vying for judicial ratification. If society and religion are this inextricable on a large scale, they're even more so on a daily, personal level. For those of us who identify as Christian, faith is the lens we use to make sense of our world. It dictates how we handle challenges in life and how we initiate and respond in our relationships. When that lens is skewed, it affects us all drastically.

Theological perversions can be so subtle. I have come to believe that unless we approach the Bible and faith with self-awareness, we risk infusing faith with our own harmful backgrounds and stories instead of allowing it to release us from them. This is what I believe "taking the Lord's name in vain" is really about, a warning to those of us rushing to justify our prejudices and vendettas with a "Christian" label instead of allowing our faith to renew our minds and soften our hearts.

Here are some theologically twisted beliefs that were built into my psyche, labeled as faith, and ingested in my identity.

Women are Created for Everyone Else First

Most women's teaching in the conservative Christian circles I have frequented is others focused. Teaching on servanthood is fine, but we have to know our audience. If most women are coming into our churches with an embodied belief that our worth is determined by men and/or achievement, even when we claim worthiness in faith, our brains haven't created the new synapses necessary to tell us we are really safe.

Yes, our worth in faith is determined by God, but God does

not hold our worth ransom the way others in our lives have. The dynamic is a 180-degree turnaround from our societal structure of worthiness; however, this isn't often explored. In my own life, this concept taught me that my worth was dictated by how valued I was by others. Never measurable, always changing. This heavily impacted what I felt I had access to and who I was as a Christian woman.

Oh so gradually, I have learned that my worth began when I was being knit together in my mother's womb. We are created *in God's image!* Yes, us, too, not just the men. We are not created to be secondary characters in our own stories. We are not created to live in our men's shadows. *We are not here for other people first.*

There isn't a women's version of the Bible that themes service, staying small and quiet, and just praying harder when we get tired. We have access to every promise, blessing, and birthright the men do. We have the same ability to accept overflowing mercy and wrap ourselves up in grace. In Christianity, there is a trap. It is so much easier to follow rules, check off boxes, and seek approval than it is to openly and honestly engage relationally and walk through the messiness of real life. We judge the pharisees in the Old Testament for doing this very thing. Grace is scary. Participating in grace requires vulnerability and courage. I have always had a static view of grace—as a noun, the thing that enables our salvation—but I'm learning that grace is also, and maybe primarily, a verb. It's an action, something we practice in communion and relationship.

We are Intrinsically Flawed

I fully believe the gospel is a love story, and for redemption to carry its full weight, the curse of sin must be given full scope of understanding. That said, I take issue with the common teaching on worthiness that focuses only on redemption and not equally on creation. The arc is always "We are bad and sinful, but *Jesus saves!*" which leaves out critical context. We were *created* for love, connection, sacredness, empathy, compassion. This is our default template. Sin is a disease that, yes, we are all born with as well, but it is the perverse imitation of these things. Sin is the promise of the short cut, quick fix, instant results that leaves us feeling empty and hollow. Sin is the story we tell ourselves, that if people knew the real us, they wouldn't like us, when in reality, we have never given them the chance to make that decision. Sin is the question of what we know in our gut to be true, "but hath God not said ..." (Genesis 3:1, NKJV). Sin isn't desire or doing things because we want to, or taking up space, or getting angry, or being passionate, or sexual, or receiving pleasure. Say it with me—We were not created for others first.

Jesus is not only/simply a redemptive story arc. Jesus is embodied restoration and healing. He *is* peace and groundedness. The metaphors He uses regularly speak to this. Jesus enforced personal boundaries throughout His ministry, and it was *part* of His ministry. Autonomy is so important to God that not only was Jesus human on earth, but He carried full autonomy here. The example we have to follow of the Trinity shows strong and sacred trust. Out of that comes full submission based on mutual goals and relationship. *This* is why we always have a choice.

Claiming Worthiness is Pride

Pride is, no question, dangerous; however, we don't always understand it. One of the Merriam-Webster definitions of pride is "excessive self-esteem," and in general day-to-day logic, this makes sense. However, pride described in the Bible is a more complex issue. An overview of original Hebrew and Greek words translated as pride shows there are actually four different but similar words used. Pride biblically refers most often to "one who is insolent, presumptuous, or arrogant, a scoffer or a mocker" (Proverbs, 21:24, NKJV). I see this today as an inability to acknowledge that we might be wrong, a lack of self-awareness and pushing our own personal agendas no matter the cost to others.

I recently participated in a workshop called Spiritual Activism 101, led by Rachael Ricketts. In the workshop, she talked about how damaging our obsession with being good and right is.

Our need to feel okay in life, to know ourselves and be known as good people often becomes a form of idolatry. Isn't that pride? The minute we feel our G&R status start to slip, we work double time to make up for it: "Well, they must just not understand my intentions," "They don't know what a good person I really am."

Even our gut reaction to vent to sympathizing friends when we're offended is just another example of us groping for validation that we are somehow justified.

That we are really good.

That we are really right.

Our drive to feel good and right often is what propels us into personal development in the first place. Sometimes, it's what pushes us to consider religion and faith. We are looking for ways to feel okay with ourselves, to drown out the rumbling thunder in the closet where we've shoved all our darkness.

It's easy to miss the nuance in faith when we talk about the need to be good and right. G&R is the lure of fundamentalism (really in any faith, not just Christianity). Fundamentalism is a dangerous solution, combining beliefs of unworthiness, perfectionism, and shame. Fundamentalism tells us we only must say the right words, wear the right clothes, listen to the right music, pray the right prayers, and live the right lives to be seen as good. I am exhausted just from writing that sentence. Living the life is even more draining.

What I love about Christianity, and one thing that has kept me in it when I've lost hope, is that it's never been about us being good or right. Being made in God's image, understanding our worth and the worth of others as human does not mean any of us are good or right. It does not mean we won't have a harmful impact on others, no matter our intentions. This is where some of the scriptures that are often misused to shame folks into compliance come in. The "doom and gloom" scriptures show us a few things.

They show us our darkness. They show us where we begin in relation to God. They show us the need for grace and redemption. The point of grace and redemption isn't to make us good and right. The point of grace and redemption is to enable relationship. We cannot stay centered in good and right and live out stories of grace and love. We can't cling to good and right and carry compassion to our dark places and shadow sides. If we can't carry compassion to our dark places, we have no understanding of how to engage others in ways that are safe for them and us. Others are only safe as long as they don't call out our darkness. Others are only safe as long as their darkness doesn't remind us too much of our own.

Pride would rather make a trite meme or comic with digs at opposition instead of sitting down with those who have different views and listening to their hearts. Sure, this could be from the root of excessive self-esteem but more regularly seems to come from fear and shame. We may have a difficult time having conversational give and take with someone who has a distorted sense of how amazing they are, but it is impossible to have an authentic exchange of ideas with a person operating out of fear, shame, and unworthiness. Pride today seems too often present in championing any cause with no care for the people behind the other side, no motivation to hear their stories and perspectives, no check to develop our own self-awareness. At its very worst, we put God's name on our pet causes and start our own crusades and holy wars.

Humility, in contrast, is openness and vulnerability. Willingness to be wrong and without shame, to expand our frames of reference. Willingness to say, "Oh, wow! I will do better here" without having to prove how or why we've made the decisions we made in the past. Our worth isn't based in being right. I think it's easy to forget that Israel expected Jesus to come as a political leader, and He didn't. They expected Him to overthrow the Roman occupation, but He didn't. Instead, He zeroed in on the heart matters, the uncomfortable truths. He uncovered the hypocrisy, the legalism, the extortion and expected His followers to deal with themselves, not Rome. We would do well to remember this. Maybe it's trite to say hurt people hurt people, but it's true. The amazing thing is that healed people heal people, and empowered people empower people.

Restoring our identities and pursuing healing are the most sacred missions. When we choose paths of grace and accept our own healing, we heal each other. When we heal each other, we heal our world.

Our world needs so much healing.

Selective Self-Acceptance

Growing up, self-acceptance was preached (there was even a catchy kids song about it), but, unfortunately, it was not modeled. We were taught self-acceptance but did not actually accept ourselves or each other when we had limitations, varying beliefs, and conflicting biblical interpretations. We preached self-acceptance but hid behind our projects. We crashed and burned out as proof of our service instead of realizing burnout is a misuse and form of disrespect of our gifts. We preached self-acceptance but still fell in line with the teachings of social patriarchy, stripping away the most powerful and nuanced parts of ourselves in an effort to be more accepted and holy.

If we are to fully honor ourselves and each other as creations of God, we must invoke grace in our messy places. Those things we are uncomfortable with in ourselves need to be honored and accepted, too. Our inability to hold space for our limitations is what creates so much self-hatred and friction in our relationships with others. When we meet someone with a worldview or experience different from our own, our natural reaction is often defensive. We want to make sure we are still okay, still worthy in their world instead of realizing their story is about them, not us.

Others' stories of trauma, others' worldviews and experiences are not our battlegrounds for worthiness. When we make their stories about us, nobody leaves feeling seen or heard. Find your worthiness for yourself, your life, but also realize if we are constantly searching for our worthiness in others' stories, it's impossible for us to show them real love.

We can pay lip service to being made in God's image and our worth is secure no matter how bad our days, weeks, or months may be, but if we don't live this out, our lives will continue to be run by anxiety, comparison, and fear of not having or being enough. Taking care of ourselves, body, mind, and soul, is a spiritual discipline. It takes concentrated effort to teach ourselves that we matter because we matter to our God. It can feel like we don't have much control over our lives, but we all have control of our actions and our reactions.

The foundation of living proactively is having an understanding of ourselves. Getting to know myself with the understanding that I am made in Imago Dei and designed exactly as intended allows me to approach my own actions, thoughts, and emotions with less judgement. Really paying attention to how I'm feeling specifically and why leads me to more measured and thoughtful responses and actions. It also gives a purpose to challenging feelings like anger and grief. While they are still painful to process, they are now directive.

Developing self-care and self-worth gets discounted as easy because it's an incredibly positive pursuit. Yes, when you start gaining ground, it feels fantastic. That doesn't mean it's remotely easy or second nature. It takes intentional and regular practice. Nothing worthwhile in life is fast, easy, or cheap. It may cost time and energy, not money, but change of any kind has a price.

Understanding our own worthiness enables us to hold space for others and their growth journeys. When we are judgmental and harsh with others, it highlights our expectations of ourselves. I have spent a lot of time and energy in fitness spaces. It's one of the easiest places to be judgmental of both ourselves and others. As I became more body positive and started approaching my health more holistically, I was able to give others who may not have the priority of spending inordinate amounts of time and energy to achieve a specific physical aesthetic more grace. I realized there is huge societal pressure and expectation to be thin, and that is not health.

"Healthy" has become a marketing scheme. I learned about the fight people of all sizes have with eating disorders. I purposely started including women of all different sizes in my social media feeds to combat the images I'm shown every day in advertising. This has benefited my mental health and allows me to hold more grace for others. Once I realized I didn't know the whole story from looking at someone, I was able to start suspending my judgements in other areas as well. What makes sense to me is not necessarily the perfect choice for them. The more grace I can hold for myself, the more I have to offer others. This is the fruit of claiming worthiness.

In *Rising Strong*, Brene Brown raises the question: "Do you think people are doing the best they can?"[1] This was so foreign to me that it took me months to process. What if people really were doing their best, and there was just more to their story than

I could see? It also put an uncomfortable spotlight on the fact that I didn't accept my own best on any given day as enough. The story I told myself was that I had to meet rigid standards to have my efforts be considered acceptable. This was particularly painful when I was dealing with depressive episodes, barely keeping my life together enough to function and show up to work every day. Self-judgement steeped in perfectionism is not actually the most helpful remedy for depression. The question became a mantra for me both when I was feeling frustrated with others and when I wanted to judge myself for not meeting my own expectations. *What if they are doing their best right now?* or *If this is my best right now, maybe I need to be okay with that.* I have gradually begun to accept the fact that my best, on any given day, is going to vary and is going to be enough. The beauty in this is that I have also gradually begun to accept that others might just be doing their best, too, and hold space for whatever that looks like.

This worthiness journey has changed not only how I view myself in faith, but how I understand God's view of women. I can't remember what my favorite bible story was as a kid, but now, one of my favorites is part of Hagar's. Hagar, an Egyptian slave, refugee, and a woman of color, is the only human recorded in the Bible to name God—and she chooses "The God who Sees." This incredible connection started in the desert through a woman. Our female lineage of faith is not second rate or in the shadows. God has been showing up for us, seeing us from the time of Hagar and Sarai, Deborah, Huldah, and Miriam.

I know this is a lot of information. But I hope my story stirs the parts of your identity you've been afraid of. We are so often afraid of the most powerful parts of ourselves. We wonder why we are overcome by stress, why we can't seem to build resilience. Meanwhile, we placate, shush, and minimize our fire. If you also participate in Christian faith, I hope you can start to untangle Jesus from what's been imprinted on you socially, whether that's from society or the church. I hope you find your wild in yourself and in your faith. I hope you find your snarl and your bite. I hope you learn to take care of yourself and love all of yourself so very well. Love the messy, love the joyful, love the powerful, and especially love the mourning. Learn yourself through these spaces, and you will be unstoppable.

Questions to Consider for Journaling and Discussion

1. Have you ever felt your identity is tied specifically to a relationship, occupation, or role?

2. How have you defined your worth?

3. Do you feel you have to fulfill specific parameters to be okay or worthy?

4. What thought patterns do you practice? Are there any you are ready to actively release?

5. What new thought patterns would you like to be mental highways with lightning-fast access?

6. What ways are you most tempted toward judgmentalism?

7. How do you treat yourself in those areas?

2

Releasing Shame

Dear Sister,

Recognizing and releasing shame has allowed me to claim and show up in life unapologetically. Sometimes things like confidence and self-esteem seem like fairytale qualities in this world designed to profit from our pain.

In this chapter, we will explore how both society and faith hand us lists of reasons we should be ashamed. I don't consider myself overly confident, but I have done the daily work of slowly insulating my sense of self-worth from these shaming and limiting messages.

I wish I could infuse this chapter with magical powers, bringing you out through the other side fully unapologetic, but that's not real life. Realistically, I hope your perspective shifts just a little. I hope you start noticing the places in your life you've handed over to shame. I hope you take a few more steps toward your fairytale, magical, unapologetic self.

Cheering you on,
Megan

Everything I've learned about my body was about someone else.
How my body related to men.
How my body related to church.
To my purity
To my value.

How I moved
How I dressed
Was never about me.

I suppose it's no small wonder
It's taken me thirty years to discover
That my body is really mine.

One of the more restrictive parts of my childhood was the restrictions on music. While I love that I got a fantastic education in classical music, I have always felt jazz in my soul. I would catch bits of it out and about as a kid but actively try to disconnect from how it felt in my body. The narrow restrictions on music and dance in my world were my first lesson that my soul expanding my ribcage and moving with rhythm was dangerous. That part of *me* was dangerous.

Shame and Sexuality

Dancing was never about the music. Friendship with the opposite sex was rarely about companionship. What I chose to wear wasn't about comfort, utility, or identity. Everything was about sexuality in some way. I never really considered my body my own while growing up. It always felt like a rental, a means to experience but not a home. There were lots of rules from various landlords. They all stemmed from keeping any expression of sensuality or sexuality under wraps. It was clear this part of me was shameful, something I had to suppress until I someday got married and gifted it to a man.

It most certainly wasn't for me.

The dangerous part of faith-based shame is how we attribute it to holiness. I hit puberty at the age of twelve and contritely confessed any sexual urges to God. I invited God's judgement for any imagined missteps. Of course, God must judge me. Of course, these urges were not meant for me. This was not a new, womanly, part of me unfurling; it was a dangerous fire to be constantly smothered. I experienced this cognitive dissonance of both wanting to grow up and be mature but also feeling intensely ashamed of my changing body.

For some reason, I thought I could write this book without talking about sex and sexuality ... but here we are. I recently read *Pure* by Linda Kay Klein, and it was intensely relatable. Linda talks about the dangers of the purity movement in evangelical Christianity. She talks about her experience and the experiences of the eighty-plus people she interviewed for her book. It's an astonishing piece of work.

A few chapters in, I had to put the book down. I was floored by how deeply embedded many of the harmful teachings were, especially the ones that hit much closer to home than expected. Linda wasn't just talking about some fringe sect of Christian faith. She was talking about me, about my friends and our experiences.

After reading *Pure*, I realized by not talking specifically about shaming sexuality, I would be doing what we've all been doing for years—continuing the silence. Keeping the shroud and extending the shame. I refuse to be part of that tradition.

I refuse to be part of a paradigm that promotes sexual disassociation[2] for women.

Once upon a time, I met a boy online. I was lonely and isolated, and he was opportunistic. He flew in from across the country to visit me. *(Chris, would like you all to know that, on no uncertain terms, this was an ex of mine, not him.)* I was naive and had no understanding of relationships past wanting someone to be close to. While he was far from experienced, he was also far from respectful. Had I any understanding that my body was mine and I made its rules, the boundaries I enforced likely would have been different.

This story is probably like many other girls' coming of age experiences. Looking back over twelve years ago and eight-plus years of marriage to Chris, what I experienced in that relationship blip of a few months was minimal and inconsequential.

But what sticks with me is the anger from having no idea I was my own.

I want to go back and tell my younger self that the line of "too far" she searched so hard for was always hers to set.

That sex is often as funny as it is sumptuous.

That, yes, intimacy will change her forever.

That all those things she feels when she hears jazz are hers.

That she doesn't owe part of herself as tribute to keep anyone in her life.

But, most importantly, that she is her own.

Why do we think teaching girls their bodies are everyone else's first will ensure their abstinence? Why do we think this will protect them? In and of itself, this invalidates their trust of themselves and understanding of their own worthiness. If I'm just keeping house in a rental, who the current owner is might not make a big difference. But if my house is *mine,* I'm going to paint the walls. I'm going to plant flowers. I might even install a security system. I am responsible for the care and keeping of *my* house. We can't teach girls their spirit is housed in a rental and expect them to learn that they are their own.

Purity culture shames women into disassociating from their sexual selves then expects an immediate awakening when they say, "I do."

Yes, yes, I sense some eyebrows raising, trying to categorize my opinions as legitimate or not based on if I condemn extramarital sex. Given that so many women have been silenced, shamed, and minimized by purity teachings, when they end up having sex isn't my concern. My concern is if they are able to be wholly invested. If they know what "yes" and "no" feel like in their bodies. If they feel safe voicing that. If they have been educated about their own anatomy and the anatomy of their potential partners. If they know how to unabashedly participate in their own pleasure.

If my understanding of faith and my own autonomy encouraged me to develop a fierce "no," I likely never would have fallen for easy flattery in the first place, even at eighteen.

If I wrote a cookbook full of tantalizing desserts, would you ask me my feelings on the sin of gluttony? If I wrote a book about managing investments, would you remind me that the pursuit/love of money and power is the root of all evil? If not, why must every discussion of sexuality center on when we choose to engage with a partner?

I can tell you why. We are ashamed.

Do you know how we can protect our families? *Lose the shame.*

Secular views of sexuality are based in the power dynamic of holding our worthiness ransom. Men's worthiness is held ransom in conquest and ownership. Women's worthiness is held ransom in desirability and being chosen. Tell me how purity culture dismantles this story? It doesn't serve men or women; yet, from what I've heard, men's teachings aren't focused on dismantling the secular mindset that women are seductive, pretty objects they can acquire if they play the game right. Obviously, I've heard less of these talks than the women's side, but the narrative focuses on just not touching the pretty objects 'til they are actually yours.

Not that women are colleagues who have immense strength

and wisdom to lend if they can be "man enough" (humble enough?) to listen.

Not that women are whole people, not prizes to be won for playing one stage of the game of life right.

Men are shamed for what they do and what they want.

Women are shamed for who we are.

Our side of these teachings is modesty. We are taught to cover up, pipe down, and hide so as not to provoke the men to fall out of line. Our worth still lies in being desirable, but we can't be *too* desirable.

Here's what I learned when I got married after a decade of hearing these messages. Sex isn't that big of a deal. I don't mean that sex isn't/can't be intimate, bonding, or incredibly pleasurable. But the amount of energy and effort that went into talking about sex in purity culture does not match the run time it gets in a normal, romantic, adult relationship. It does match the run time secular society gives it, though.

Here's the thing—sex sells because of unhealthy and limiting worthiness dynamics. Sex is selling worthiness, belonging, and security, not orgasms. It's telling men they can be *real men* and have the sexy woman prize by buying the cologne or car. It's telling women they can be the sexy woman prize by becoming less and less of themselves.

There was a popular term when I was young about the dangers of dating (coined by Josh Harris in *I Kissed Dating Goodbye*). It was "giving your heart away," the illustration that each person you've dated or fell for stole a piece of your heart. The more pieces of your heart you gave away before you married, the less would be left for your future spouse. It's ironic that this dysfunctional mindset is supposed to be promoting wholeness.

I was so afraid to feel and lose myself, I had no idea who I was.

Brene Brown PhD LMSW has been researching and teaching on shame for over sixteen years, and, originally, instead of writing this chapter, I really just wanted to put a page in with references to four of her books. However, the more I do this work, the more I realize we need to see *each other* walking through these messy spaces. I am sharing Brene's definition of shame, though: "The intensely painful feeling or experience of believing that we are flawed and therefore unworthy of love and belonging."[3]

Even that short story of giving your heart away is laced with shame and emotional bullying. The message: You will be worth less the more you love.

If you are interested in further research, Brene's books are listed in the "Recommended Reading" appendix in the back of this book. Her books will give you a comprehensive understanding of what shame is. How we manage shame is an integral part of our ability to flourish. Brene unpacks all this and backs it up with academic data. Her books are research based but not at all challenging to read or inaccessible.

My own reduction of shame after years of reading and personal work is that shame presents the feeling that everything about who I am is wrong. Sound familiar from the "Worthiness" chapter? Shame decimates our worthiness, and without understanding worthiness, it's nearly impossible to combat shame.

Shame and Christianity

In the Bible, there is no point where I see shame used by God. The first mention of shame biblically was when Adam and Eve knew they were naked "and were ashamed." Their nakedness is not the focus of this verse, but how they felt about it. God calls out for them, asking, "Where are you?" knowing something cataclysmic happened to sever their intimacy. Shame and unworthiness have been destroying our ability to hold intimate relationships with God and each other since the Garden of Eden.

Assuming our bodies are inherently sexual is where shaming starts. We judge the world for making "sexualized" children's toys but then sexualize everything in our homes.

"Oh, sweetie, you can't wear that."

"Oh, honey, don't dance like that."

Or we make comments about our girls like:

"She's *never* dating!"

"You'll have to beat the boys off with a stick when she gets older!"

Ironically, the things we do and say to try and minimize sexuality often end up centering it. It's the shadow behind every rule, at least for women and girls. By focusing so intently on sexualization, we teach our girls that this is where their worth really lies, lock step with every marketing message they are targeted with.

My friend Heather shared her experience of religious shame with me:

> *When I got divorced, my father said, "Well, I hope you're happy being single for the rest of your life because no good Christian man is going to marry you." It's constant shame. You're not good enough if you've ever kissed a guy or looked at a guy. It's just repeating you're not worthy, you're not worthy, you're not worthy. It took a long time for me to go from not being worthy to deciding anyone didn't deserve me. That didn't happen until a few months ago.*
>
> *I didn't think I would ever get married again after I got divorced, but I married Joe because I was pregnant. I still didn't feel worthy to be his wife. I felt like he did me a favor. I didn't feel I had the right to want anything or*

disagree. Finally, a few months ago, I decided to stop that, and I don't think he knew what to do.

I decided that if he was going to treat our marriage like he was doing me a favor, I didn't want to continue. I actually am worth something, and if people don't want to be with me, they don't have to be. I told him, "If you want to be my husband, be my husband; otherwise, don't do me any favors." It shocked me to say that, but it took me until I was almost thirty to figure that out. Now, we are better than ever because I finally have some self-respect.

Things get even more complicated when girls grow up and inevitably experience harassment or worse.

The first time I experienced harassment from someone I knew, I thought I'd heard him wrong. I spent days doubting the "no" in my body, my senses, and my intuition. The next time it happened, I was sure. But maybe I could control the situation to keep it from happening again. I had a pattern to observe. The third, fourth, and fifth times were an uncomfortable dance of attempting to avoid harassment and it finding me anyway.

It wasn't just the comments made about my body, clothing, or food. It was how he talked about other women. Derogatory remarks about women his own age cloaked as humor. (They were obviously past their "prime," even though his desirability apparently remained evergreen.) I was acceptable in a twisted sense, but that couldn't last forever. Even though my professional skills were excellent, it was clear where the bulk of my worth lay in his eyes at that time.

To make things more complicated, when he wasn't misogynistic, he was affable and charming, the quinnessential "good guy." How was I to know where the line was, anyway? How much should I put up with in the name of friendly banter of someone "well intentioned"? If I could coach my past self through this, I would remind her of two things: She sets the line, always, and the impact of someone's actions always outweighs their intentions. How many victims have been silenced by assurances of good intentions on the part of aggressors? Too many.

My friend Heather's brushes with harassment affected her in a different way:

> *In therapy, we discussed that it seemed like all the girls I knew were molested by their brothers or other men. They would tell me to be glad I didn't have a brother. As I got older, I associated molestation and abuse with being something that happened to pretty girls. It was a marker of desirability. When it happened to people close to me, I started wondering what was wrong with me. At work, I was twenty-two or twenty-three, and my supervisor had sexual harassment claims against him from every other girl there except me. I was asked why I didn't report him, and it was because he'd never done anything. I had feelings of shame and worthlessness because I thought I wasn't even pretty enough to get harassed. I actually still know him, and I finally got the courage to say, "I have no interest in you and don't come near me, but why not me?" And he said, "I knew you would talk." So that made me feel so much better. That was big for me. I had such a complex.*

I am proud of reporting my harassment because it was one of the first major boundaries I drew in my life.

I have chalked this experience up to living as a woman for years, and really, it's most women's story. It's the light, happy ending, easy version of most women's stories. I considered my case closed long ago.

Recently, it came up in conversation between Chris and me in reference to my personal growth journey. We pieced together that these years of sporadic harassment is when I started hiding. I tossed the boots that were commented on every time I wore them (a sultry two-and-a-half-inch heel). I hid behind oversized jackets and clothes. The shame of harassment became my strongest association with my sexuality. When I got dressed, it was first about if what I wore would be more likely to garner unsolicited comments and second about what I wanted. It was easiest to just shut down.

It's concerning that when we layer common Christian teachings and beliefs over experiencing harassment, there's no contrasting voice. Christian tradition has always seen women's sexuality as shameful, dangerous, and for someone else. Our participation in our pleasure is a bonus feature at best. Sexuality is for men; relational connection is for women. If you don't fall in these lines, there is a special Christian version of slut shaming that often follows. (Harlot and Jezebel are usually the preferred Christianese for "ho.") Harassment can feel like a sinister confirmation at best or divine judgement at worst.

Sexuality and sensuality are supposed to magically spring up in marriage and definitely nowhere else, ever. Somehow, we women are supposed to preserve our sexual identity in this hostile environment but only to share with a husband. This thing we are born with isn't even primarily for us. When this is our experience of sexuality, what is the point?

Imagine with me if our daughters and girls were so sure of their identity and worth that flattery always fell flat. If we encouraged them to listen to their gut instincts and hone their intuition so they could side-step dangerous situations and people. If those in Christian faith traditions knew their sensuality and sexuality were God-given parts of themselves they chose to share intimately at the right time. If we trusted God in them to know when that time was. If they were more focused on growing into their gifts than how they showed up in the world. For this to happen, though, we have to trust our girls, and we have to trust God.

Shame as Armor

We'll explore these dynamics in more detail in the "Patriarchy" chapter—this is equally based in shame and systems of patriarchy. However, another reason we focus so much on female sexuality is that we want to protect our girls. We know the statistics. One in three women have been victims of sexual assault or harassment. We know the women, we know the stories. We have all measured the threat in footsteps behind us, held our keys between our fingers as we walked to our cars, had set check-ins with friends when we went to meet a date for the first time. This is our life, yet we tell our girls to shut down, hoping it won't be theirs. We want control. If we can only hide our girls somehow, maybe they won't experience what we have. Maybe they'll be safe in the world.

But how can they be safe from what we've never prepared them for? Innocence is not armor.

In Christianity, shame and relational disconnection are a main component of the curse of sin, causing separation from God and each other. Unfortunately, living in a world infected with shame, it's nearly impossible to eradicate from our relationships with others, God, and ourselves. The example given of a shameless relationship is that of Jesus and God the Father. Full trust and vulnerability cannot be accomplished unless we actively affirm our worthiness and value of each other no matter our differences.

We become so accustomed to living with shame and navigating around our vulnerable places that it camouflages easily. I often think back to when I was a very little girl, and I reveled in being loved. I was proud of my ideas and not afraid of what anyone thought. This didn't last long, of course. My reactions to criticism and being made fun of were shutting down and questioning my worth. This is shame. That gut feeling of being rejected for who we are and desperately trying to change to be more palatable to others. We all have these stories of cringeworthy rejection and deeply painful betrayals we remember vividly. This is shame. Shame is a deep-seated fear of vulnerability, of being seen for who we are then being rejected. The sin of shame is what leads God to gently prod us with "Why are you hiding?" (Genesis 3:8, NKJV).

My friend Kelly shared her experience with shame:

> *I didn't understand the effect that shame had on me. I didn't understand that I was essentially in a prison because of it. I didn't understand that my own thinking and thought processes were shame based. So that whole exploration over the last couple years, it was literally two or three years of "Oh, wow, I didn't even realize this was happening in my head! Where did that come from? Where did I learn that?" Then systematically going through childhood, and teenage years, and the church, and leadership in the church. It's a process. It's still a process. I feel like it's a stronghold. Even understanding what shame really is and how insidious it can be is a journey. There are things people can say to you as a child, and you don't even realize how it imposes that kind of thought process on you.*

Shame as a Marketing Ploy

Materialistic society too often utilizes shame-based structures, creating a false dichotomy of the life you could have if you only buy this shirt, makeup, car, house, or beer. *Then* you will be happy, *then* you will be worthy, *then* you will be accepted—and seen. The sale is in the illusion of experience, the new bathing suit to make your beach vacation perfect when, in reality, the beauty of it is in the sun, the water, and those you're there with. The beer ad sells us connection. If we buy it, we will naturally be sharing with friends on the beach or in a bar, when, in reality, we will buy it and drink at home alone. We chase after things to make us okay, to make our lives better, to numb the intense pain of shame and unworthiness, and all it does is steal our energy, money, and belief in our worth when we already have access to everything we need.

Even worse, numbing up turns off our ability to connect. The sad thing is if we took a beat and looked around, what we really want is what we give up to chase the illusion of perfection. Unfortunately, often the church follows suit here. Instead of sharing the wealth of blessing, peace, connection, and life available to us through our faith, we feel the need to sell Jesus using shame, unworthiness, and fear.

I believe every sermon we hear telling us of our unrighteousness, our unworthiness, how we will never be enough on our own in life, needs to spend equal time reminding us of our origin story, or it feeds the problem. There is nothing more dangerous than hearing words of shame from a pulpit intended to save us from it. If we are telling the redemption story, we need to include the beginning. We need to talk about creation, we need to read the psalms and look at the intimate and shame-free relationships held by women and men of faith in the Bible. Then talk about the fall of sin, then talk about the dangers of severing relational connection with God and each other and, finally, redemption, resolution, grace, and mercy.

Jesus isn't something we can package up and squeeze into our societal narrative of what religion should look like. He is wilder and more fierce than that. He is deep, satisfying, gentle, and dangerous. He presents us with the full spectrum of relationship we have been too afraid to stop and consider because it's vulnerable, and it's gritty. Jesus isn't shiny; He isn't a quick fix. He knows the whole story, and when we let our guard down, when we stop fighting our shame and fear, that's when we can hear Him.

It's true that we are mired in sin, shame, and patriarchal systems. The challenge is for the church to be the example of another way. Others should want the groundedness, peace, and love that we share. *That* is our witness. Jesus did not bow to the order of religious society or Roman society. He initiated a new order, a new kingdom here on earth. He came so we could have and share abundant life. Is that the story we are living?

The Antidote

The antidote to shame, according to Brene's work, is vulnerability. The concept of vulnerability often elicits a visceral cringe. When I was first introduced to the idea of vulnerability as a component of connection, I termed it a "dysfunction yard sale" in my journal. Now, to me, vulnerability just means taking that risk to be authentically seen by and see others. Vulnerability means dropping the list of roles and requirements that I felt I had to keep up to be okay. Vulnerability is just showing up as whatever grace through faith looks like in me on any given day. Vulnerability is risking others seeing the real, authentic versions of ourselves and leaving the responsibility of what they think about us with them.

I have seen the power of vulnerable authenticity evidenced in my own life. Shame loses its grip when we talk about it openly, when we brave the possibility of rejection to share connection.

I've heard it said that preaching the "softer" side of faith lets us off the hook for our sins. But if we are to truly live in deep connection with God and each other and we are to truly love our neighbors as ourselves, if we are to actually clothe the naked and feed the hungry, we have a lot of work to do and sin to address. We need to reckon with our shame, with our fear, and with the parts of ourselves intertwined in patriarchal systems. These are the things that get in the way of our relationships and faith.

Similarly, I've heard that focusing on self-discovery, identity, and self-care is selfish. The answer is just to focus on Jesus. I believe in focusing on Jesus. I also believe that not getting to know ourselves through the eyes of our Creator is dangerous for ourselves and others. If what people think about us is really about them, the converse is also true.

What we think about other people is really about us. We learn physical self-awareness from a young age. We start toddling around, navigating stairs and sharp corners of tables and eventually graduate to operating complex heavy machinery like cars. Some of us go on to even more study. We fly planes. In the medical community, we use arthroscopic equipment as surgeons and needles that, if inserted into the spine with a smidge of the wrong pressure or location, could cause paralysis to a patient. Not getting to know ourselves emotionally is like trying to back out of our driveways with our eyes shut. Teaching others anything without having self-awareness is like administering a spinal injection without going to medical school. If we want to interact safely with our world and others, we need to put as much time into getting to know the boundaries of our inner worlds as we do our physical worlds. When we refuse to get to know ourselves well, we cause additional harm to others. We project onto them our insecurities, frustrations, and judgements. Prioritizing self-discovery and personal boundaries is not selfish; it's emotional hygiene.

I used to see self-awareness as a defense. I was painfully aware and ashamed of my "flaws." I used a convoluted version of self-awareness to sweep everything I didn't like about myself into my metaphorical closet and barricade the door so no one could ever see inside.

Self-awareness was about camouflaging my weaknesses to win the approval and acceptance of others. I think this version is encouraged in many churches. We are taught to be introspective about a very specific list of sins. But so often, we shrink from the work of really getting to know ourselves and uncovering our strengths and giftings as well as our actual dark spaces.

It took me years to prioritize uncovering the woman I was meant to be. I was so afraid of who I would become if I actually got to know myself. Awareness brings reckoning we are often not ready for. We don't want to dig too deep because we are afraid of what we might find. We spend so much energy keeping our baddies in the closet out of sight, that we don't have any left to explore new horizons.

To find myself, I had to wade through the muck of Christian codependence and expectation. I had to cut through thick smog clouding the truth of who I was created to be. The only way I could venture into the unknown wild of my psyche was with the decision that I would accept whatever I found without judgement. Self-discovery and self-compassion have to go hand in hand. This also meant gradually tearing down the barricades and unpacking my closet of Big Bad. It meant sitting with my shadow side and getting to know the ins and outs of my personal darkness.

Entering darkness in compassion has been a new experience for me. Instead of going in ready to do battle and push back a front line, I enter my dark places gently and with respect for what they have to teach me.

I struggle to rectify the version of God taught by many men who are yelling to drown out the rolling thunder of their personal darknesses with the God I know who always meets me in mine.

Who whispers through my hurricane, "Be still and know."

Questions to Consider for Journaling and Discussion

1. When do you first remember experiencing shame, feeling that who you are as a person isn't okay?

2. What coping skills did you develop to shield yourself from or work through those feelings of shame? Did they lead you into vulnerability and community or exclude you from it?

3. Have you ever shamed others as an attempt to change their behavior?

3

Releasing Scarcity

Dear Sister,

Now that we've explored where we place our worthiness and detoxed from the shameful messages we're bombarded with, it's time to evaluate what having and being enough means in our lives.

Even when we understand our intrinsic worth and unapologetically advocate for our needs, we can be incapacitated by the not ever enough (scarcity) monster. The monster attacks our sense of security physically and emotionally.

The most sinister side of the scarcity monster colors and shifts how we view others. It whispers that their plenty must equal our lack. That sharing enough means we must want. This idea saturates everything from marketing messages to political speeches and even legislation.

I'd love to solve all the inequities that taught us scarcity is a viable coping skill, but I'll settle for raising awareness. I'll settle for a conversation about what enough can look like. I'll hope we can build a world where an army of women support and advocate for each other to always have enough.

Always beside you on this journey,
Megan

Enough used to feel strained.
Just barely getting what I need.
Now Enough feels abundant.
Always waiting to be claimed.

When we starve ourselves
Of connection
Of love
Of creative work
Enough seems always out of reach
We feel we must drink the world dry to quench our thirst.
When fed well, we only need a sip.

I've done a lot of sifting, looking for where certain beliefs started. I'm not just talking about theology. I'm talking about the things that I believe so intrinsically that they create the responses of my brain and body before I know what's happening. I think sometimes, when we say "belief," we mean "mentally assent." That's one kind of belief, but there's another.

There are beliefs that run so deep our bodies acknowledge them as truth. This is the hard part about these three chapters. Often, what we believe about shame, scarcity, and patriarchy, run so deep they are embodied.

This doesn't mean we can't change them if we decide they don't represent a whole and healed version of ourselves. It just means they feel automatic. Evaluating, understanding, and effecting change to core beliefs takes incredible intention and energy. It is also worth it.

For as long as I can remember, I've been a worst-case-scenario planner. This can be helpful in moderation. It's good to have a rainy day fund in case something breaks in your house or you lose your job. Having plans for everyone in my life leaving me points to a deeper rift. I've learned it can also be a symptom of PTSD. In case you were wondering, my plan was to live out of a converted van or mini-camper and travel with my dog taking pictures and doing odd jobs. I mean, as far as worst case scenarios go, that isn't terrible, right?

I remember the first time I admitted to Chris that I do this. He looked at me like I was from another planet, and I realized everyone doesn't have in-case-of-abandonment plans.

It's taken me a long time to work out where this started for me. While there have been ups and downs in my family relationships, I never thought they would leave me.

All clues point to this being based in spiritual trauma. While my family shifted through a few varied (but related) evangelical denominations, there was a constant. People spoke in hushed tones about "church splits." Being kicked out, disfellowshipped, or excommunicated from a church community was one of the most shameful experiences you could have. In my family's case, this never happened officially. That said, we had several situations that showed me as a child that when people misunderstand or disagree with you, especially about faith beliefs, the results can be cataclysmic.

Spiritual Trauma

I remember as a baby empath riding out feelings of joy and closeness around me, only to soon be followed by those of disillusionment and betrayal. I decided very early that I didn't trust anyone, especially other Christians. Even now, you see hotly debated flash points over different interpretations of theology. Two mutual friends of mine first memorable exchange was a shouting match outside a church building about the theological validity of potluck dinners. It's an amusing anecdote but also points to the deeper problem. It's easy to lose perspective. We have very real, pressing needs to meet in our communities and world, but instead, so often, we spend our time debating what the Bible says about potluck dinners or what kind of music is appropriate in a worship service. Attacks often go past debate quickly and try to undermine the validity and worthiness of the person in opposition. Invalidate the person to invalidate the message.

These are cruel games. Is it any wonder we have problems loving those who don't share our faith when we can't even love each other well?

Fear of abandonment brought friends to confirm and mobilize this belief in my life. Fear of not being enough. Fear of being too much. Fear of not having enough—money, time, connection, love, or joy. Fear of being misunderstood. Fear of darkness in myself and in others.

In *Daring Greatly*, Brene Brown PhD LMSW defines this concept of "scarcity" like this: "Scarcity is the 'never enough' problem. The word scarce is from the Old Norman French *scars*, meaning 'restricted in quantity' (c. 1300). Scarcity thrives in a culture where everyone is hyper aware of lack." [4]

She goes on to detail how the minutiae of our lives revolve around this structure of restriction and limited resources. We are constantly calculating our needs and wants as well as others' needs and wants. This is how we decide if we have or if we are enough. Do we have enough sleep, time, love, connection? Do we have enough money? What defines enough, and what defines satisfaction?

Brene says: "Worrying about scarcity is our culture's version of post-traumatic stress. It happens when we've been through too much, and rather than coming together to heal (which requires vulnerability), we're angry and scared and at each other's throats."[5]

Scarcity in Society & Faith

Socially, this is fed by our culture of consumerism, which teaches us that we need things to fill the holes in our lives. A cream for our wrinkles, wraps for our cellulite, brownies, ice cream, Netflix, and wine to numb out our really bad days. We are sold this idea that if we get the perfect mix of products, we can buy happiness and fulfillment. This feeds into our scarcity dilemma because if we aren't fulfilled and happy, we don't have enough or the perfect collection of *things*.

Fear and scarcity are also at the heart of the fall of humanity in Christian faith. The lie that Eve believed was the lie that she could have and needed more when she already lived in paradise. She was sold the magic potion of "being like God" when we already know she was made in God's image. The lie was lack, scarcity. A swindler selling us what we already have. There are many ways the spirit of fear can manifest, but I think this is one of the most pervasive and subtle. It can feel like anything from unease to a dire need of some *thing* to make our lives better, tolerable, or whole. It makes us lash out at those who need us and those we need. Even worse, we start to isolate ourselves, brick by brick building our own cells of disconnection.

In Philippians 4:19 (The Message), Paul just basks in enough: "You can be sure that God will take care of everything you need, his generosity exceeding even yours in the glory that pours from Jesus. Our God and Father abounds in glory that just pours out into eternity. Yes."

Jesus is recorded in both Luke 12:27 and Matthew 6:25 contrasting the care and provision given in nature with the intimate knowledge, love, and provision we have in relationship with God. He also talks about the "good gifts" God gives.

In the Old Testament, we have stories of miraculous provision. In 1 Kings 17:7-13, a widow, who traditionally would have been the most destitute as she had no one to provide for her, in a time of famine no less, is chosen to not only provide for Elijah, but also experience miraculous provision of enough.

In Exodus 16, God provides manna and quail for the Israelites and instructs them to take only what they need, not more. When some tried to keep it overnight, not only did it spoil, but they were rebuked. God supplied their needs daily, a constant reminder that God is perpetually enough.

I live in one of the wealthiest countries in the world, yet people here often seem the least fulfilled. Yes, America is a land of opportunity, but so often, instead of gathering manna in our lives and looking for the daily reminder and provision that we are held, we are secure, we are connected and loved, we try to gather and store up for fear that we will experience lack. Our belief in not enough taints even our biggest achievements and victories for fear they will vanish.

I have experienced this in my own life in many different ways. Anxiety loves telling me stories about my life that paint it in the direst of settings. Even beautiful moments are but a mirage, set up to expose me somehow when they come crashing down the minute I trust them. Trusting the good in God is a practice for me. I must remember that I have a Divine Parent who gives *good gifts* to their children and has given me the spirit of love, and of power, and of a sound mind.

The not-ever-enough monster circles, waiting for some kind of loss in my life. "See?" it seethes. "There is no bounty. Your worst fears are justified. Perhaps this happened because you were not enough to deserve peace in your life. You are not worthy of feeling safe." The lie the monster weaves is not just about now, but about the future, too. Telling me that even when things are going well, I won't be able to shake the shadows that lurk behind my blessings.

But the monster has a secret; it's all smoke and shadow. Even the warrior and veteran fall prey to its illusion. We light our way by reveling in small daily moments. Unexpected provisions and confirmation of mission remind us that we are not alone. No matter the challenge, we are and have enough.

Embodying Enough

I'm a firm believer that we can all mentally process what is true and what we should be doing, but if we don't address the reasons we do what we do and learn to embody change, there will be no progress for any of us.

Brene's point that scarcity is a response to trauma is key. Scarcity is a default way of coping most of us have learned at some point, often when we were kids. We didn't have all the information to process change or loss in our lives in healthy ways. Maybe we experienced childhood trauma. Maybe we survived abuse, bullying, mental illness of ourselves or of a parent.

Maybe you're reading this and feel I don't get your life. Maybe lack and loss feel like siblings you grew up with who still drain your bank account and leave you exhausted, depleted, and never able to get out of survival mode. Maybe you have physical symptoms that embody what life has handed you like hypertension and anxiety. Maybe the thought of feeling safe and secure seems so out of reach that it's laughable. I want you to know that I see you. Whatever life has handed you, you are worthy and deserving of safety, peace, and rest. I believe that the God of Enough sees you, too. I want to be clear—I'm not promoting a prosperity gospel here. I'm not saying life won't be hard or that our limits and capacity won't be tested. Some of those who professed faith and followed God in the Bible spent a lifetime wandering in the wilderness under hostile occupation or even worse—servitude. Deliverance comes but not always when or how we would like it to. Lack and loss are real life things we must find ways to cope with. We don't get to decide if they visit us or live with us, but we can decide how to respond to them.

I see enough as not only something to claim for myself but for our collective. Believing in enough for myself comes with a commitment to making sure my sisters have enough, too. It means I'm committed to using whatever influence I have to create a world where we all experience enough. I'm not just talking about my sisterhood here in the U.S.; I'm talking about the women in the global south, where being born female is often still an invitation to violence at best and an early death sentence at worst. We haven't arrived until we have all arrived.

As long as 132 million girls in the global south don't have access to education, we haven't arrived.[6]

As long as indigenous women are 3-3.5 times more likely to go missing as the rest of the female population, and as long as ninety percent of them experience sexual assault (and eighty-six percent of them experience assault at the hands of nontribal members),[6] we haven't arrived.

As long as our black sisters have the highest maternal mortality rate in the U.S.,[7] we haven't arrived.

As long as our American and European cultures bombard us with constant messages of shame about our bodies, leaving seventy-five percent of women with disordered eating and body dysmorphia,[8] we haven't arrived.

The greatest gift we have been given is the gift of each other, the gift of relationship and community. But if we aren't taking action against these issues and more, we are failing our sisterhood. These are sharp, painful reminders of constant lack and loss in our world. We need to learn how to find enough in our lives, but we also need to learn how to back up our thoughts and prayers for those in crisis with solidarity and action.

I fully believe all our past selves did the best they could with the information they had at the time. I'm not here to tell survivors they're doing it wrong. I'm just here to ask, if you identify with this chapter at all, how have your current beliefs served you? What fruit do they carry in your life? Do they open doors for you, create new connections, or do they isolate you?

If your experience of scarcity is anything like mine, maybe it's time all our coping skills got an upgrade.

Just like we have embodied scarcity in our responses to hard things in our lives, we need to learn how to embody our new skill sets, too. It takes time. Some of us have held scarcity as a security blanket for ten, twenty, or fifty years. One month of writing mantras (or bible verses) on your mirror isn't going to undo that.

It's easy to talk about change. It's harder to—you know—actually do it.

I don't want you to leave this book on a bookshelf or nightstand, in your car, or the donation box without feeling like you had tangible ways to live into it.

Only you can find what coping skills will help release the vice grip of scarcity, but I will share a few of mine. The positive coping skills we need are often determined by how we've interacted with scarcity most. Since scarcity is a response, we must look at where it began.

I've talked a lot about my struggles with worthiness and identity. At one point, I felt my identity depended on obtaining the perfect mix of *things*. That wearing the t-shirt, dress, heels, or brand, made me the girl marketing schemes had whipped up in my head. This really is a brilliant trick because, at the end of the day, I hadn't changed and was just convinced I hadn't yet found the magical right things.

When you're playing a part, no one can know the real you. It's the most isolating catch 22. I needed the things to feel like I belonged but couldn't actually belong without setting them aside. Doing the work I described in "Finding Worthiness" allowed me to release this version of scarcity. Once I was secure in my identity, no matter what I (or my house) looked like, the pull was gone.

I've also responded to change and impermanence in scarcity. I'm a routine-oriented person. I can eat the same thing for lunch and wear the same clothes (I wash them) for a month or two without getting bored. Those who follow me on social media are familiar with my favorite fuzzy robe. I get up at the same time every day, and my routine involves breakfast, coffee, and options including writing, reading, and getting ready for my day. I don't like change.

I also have an unrealistic expectation that the things and people in my life will last forever. For a long time, I expected things like friendships, church communities, jobs, and hobbies to all be forever. Are you seeing a problem yet, any ways in which life doesn't play by my rigid rules? My response to anything in my world changing in unexpected ways was always a lockdown or hustling harder to keep things the same. This was impossible and exhausting.

I found the antidote to this form of scarcity in nature. All of life has seasons. The key is knowing what season we are in. Nothing in nature is static or unchanging. Even the biggest trees are slowly adding rings, taking up a little more space in the world. I still don't like change, but I've acknowledged its elemental nature. I used to believe I could only function in my carefully constructed and controlled world. But tidal waves of change have taught me I'm so much stronger than I gave myself credit for, and sometimes change even brings something beautiful.

Once we work to intentionally release the belief of constant lack, we can work to build places of healing for ourselves and others.

In "Releasing Shame," we talked about getting to know ourselves including our shadow sides. This is the background work we must do to create places of healing. We aren't called to hand out crosses to hang on the closet doors where our Big Bad lives. We are called to painstakingly unpack the closets and show others it's safe to peek into their own. If we don't do this work, others will, at some point, fall over the baggage we refuse to unpack.

This can sound like a lot of work, and it is. The wonderful thing is that just by doing this work and sharing our journeys, we can plant vibrant, loving communities. Just maybe those communities can help heal our world.

"There is no room in love for fear. Well-formed love banishes fear. Since fear is crippling, a fearful life—fear of death, fear of judgment—is one not yet fully formed in love" (1John 4:18, The Message).

Questions to Consider for Journaling and Discussion

1. How does the spirit of fear/scarcity show up in my life?

2. Where do I feel constrained or lack in my life?

3. What or who am I jealous of?

4. What do I feel I need to be okay that I'm not getting?

5. What am I most afraid of losing?

6. How would I fill in the blank: not _____ enough when talking about myself and my life?

7. What fruit/results of my belief patterns do I see in my life?

8. How does God show up for me in my life?

9. How have I experienced enough in my life?

4

Releasing Patriarchy

Dear Sister,

For twenty-seven years, I suppressed a powerful part of my identity. My femininity was on lockdown. I was submerged in cultures and subcultures that discounted the callings, voices, and needs of their women. I saw my gender primarily as a liability and challenge to overcome.

We *must* have this conversation about the role patriarchal systems play in our lives and communities. They not only undermine the flourishing of women and girls; they also undermine the emotional development and expression of our men and boys.

This chapter is for everybody, and we need all hands on deck. Empowered and emboldened women don't just empower other women; we transform communities. If you haven't examined the role patriarchy has played in your life and community before, I hope this chapter gives you the tools to take that journey. If you're already with me, I hope it gives you affirmation and reminds you we're in this together.

Walking with you,
Megan

I used to dislike the word "sister" as a term for anyone other than my flesh-and-blood relative. It felt like just another vestige of archaic, unrelatable religion that had little to no impact on my actual life or faith. I also didn't have very many close female friendships and didn't really think I needed them. My own understanding and acceptance of my femininity was limited and stunted. My chosen coping skill for dealing with all the challenges and hardships of being a woman was to give as little space as possible to female energy in my life.

Aren't men better/faster/stronger anyway? Why would I ever value intuition or emotion over logic? The idea of pregnancy and childbirth terrified me, and I felt that menstruation was just a monthly reminder that my biology got the really raw (and bloody) end of the deal. I felt disconnected relationally, constantly overwhelmed and exhausted, always hustling and grinding for my worth.

I resented being born a woman. Don't get me wrong, I never felt like I was anything but female; however, from the time I was a kid, I saw the vast difference in what was available to and expected of me versus what was available to and expected of my male friends.

At homeschool conferences, the programs for young boys included outdoorsy and athletic challenges while I was relegated to sitting indoors all day listening to speakers and doing craft projects. My family never pushed me specifically toward societal roles; however, the roles still permeated our social circles. The most damaging part of this was faith leaders labeling them as holy. If I wanted to be valuable to God, I needed to fall in line.

Biologically, I resented the weighty responsibility on my shoulders to make decisions about child bearing. I resented not having any say in whether I am the one most affected by the decision to bring new life into the world. I used to joke that I thought I would make a great dad. The all-encompassing role of motherhood, including the likely decimation of my body, sounded like a dystopian reality to me. This is what I associated with being female.

The first time I remember being happy to be a woman was January 21, 2017. I was twenty-seven years old before I had an experience that made me think maybe all the pain and disadvantages are worth the trouble and fight. Something about being at the Women's March in Hartford, CT put femininity in a new light for me. I went to interview attendees for a photo documentary project, but I also knew history was happening. I wanted to see it, document it, and be immersed in it. Talking to all these amazing people there for myriad reasons started painting a new picture in my mind. I realized that by discounting and begrudging my femininity, I was refusing to tap into the full gifting and power of my identity.

Up until that day, my goal was to make peace with the disadvantages of being female. After, my goal became unlocking the power in my femininity I had discounted and ignored.

This is the story of internalized patriarchy in my life. In our conservative homeschool circles, motherhood was glorified as the apex of Christian femininity; however, my inner empath could always see through to the trapped, overwhelmed, and exhausted women behind the ideal that was sold. Of course, not all of them were. We were (are) blessed to know some stellar women, some of who I was in complete awe of as a child. Unfortunately, this was not the norm.

The term patriarchy is thrown around a lot right now. Generally defined, patriarchy means "**A system of society or government** in which the father or eldest male is head of the family and descent is traced through the male line. **A system of society or government** in which men hold the power and women are largely excluded from it. **A society or community** organized on patriarchal lines."[9]

The first thing I want to point out, before we dig into this chapter further, are the words in bold in the definition. Patriarchy is a system. It is a power dynamic and structure that has been enforced in various ways for millennia. This is not about men being evil, awful, horrible people. This is about what happens when systems of society and government are set up with a vast imbalance of power. This imbalance is bad for all of us, men included.

The other fundamental thing to remember as we move forward is that patriarchy isn't static. It is a continuum. We start with blatant suppression of women. Sexual harassment, not hiring women based on their likelihood of having or being needed by their families, refusing to speak to them or acknowledge their presence, violence against women, treating women as property instead of people, not allowing women to vote or own property, and the overt gendercide still happening in many countries. As we move further along, however, it becomes more insidious. We start to see a lack of celebration and empowerment of women. The acceptance that men have always filled certain roles and spaces, and that's just how things are.

Sometimes this surfaces (especially in Christian circles) in the statement that "men and women just have different gifts." Obviously, men and women are not the same, but I recently realized why this phrase bothers me so deeply. For generations, women have been silenced and subjugated. Our gifts and strengths have been buried. So tell me what those drawing this conclusion know of our gifts? Tell me what they know of our resilience and our leadership? What do they know of our persistence?

Strengthen our voices, then we can share discussion of variance in gifting. Train women in leadership, then marvel at their unique perspectives. But don't judge the gifting and brilliance of womankind based on a society that has spent millennia showering men with opportunity and women with deprivation.

Many of us are so used to living with some level of patriarchy, it feels normal.

My personal definition of patriarchy is inequality and inequity of women in any space. At its core, the system of patriarchy promises power to men who play the game perfectly, and it promises security to the women. The imbalance is clear here. In the "perfect world," according to patriarchy, men have success and women have safety. What's the American dream of a house with a white picket fence anyway? For women, it can typify a safe and nurturing environment. For men, in the realm of patriarchy, it can be the pretty box where they keep their prize possessions, proof of their worthiness. It looks like we have the same dream, and we wonder why we can't understand each other when we get there.

My patriarchy alarm goes off when I notice things like:

- Lack of diversity and women in an industry, committee, or place of power
- No path for women and girls to follow into leadership spaces
- Feeling like the thoughts, opinions, and feelings of myself and other women are unwelcome or not legitimate because of our gender
- Feeling like the worth of myself or other women is dependent on how we present ourselves and how valued we are by the men in our lives
- Feeling like my voice and message must be carefully constructed and crafted to gain the approval of men
- A culture of scarcity—limited resources—forcing women to compete for the attention and blessings of the men in their lives, feeling like if other women win they must be losing

- Defining "woman" with any specific list of attributes because we are vast and diverse enough to encompass any and all of them
- Defining "man" or "masculine" with any specific list of attributes because men are vast and diverse enough to encompass any and all of them
- Shaming men for attributes that patriarchy tells us are feminine like nurturance and caretaking
- The silence created by the patriarchal version of "masculinity" for men around mental health and emotional well-being
- Shaming men by calling them names associated with girls and women
- An expectation of men to always provide and lead, even if that's not in their gifting or skills
- Associating male success with degrading women and treating them as objects
- Assuming men have no self-control or dignity, and this is the reason behind assault and harassment
- Shaming men for listening to and standing up for women, for gaining wisdom from women

Patriarchy in Real Life

I have always been acutely aware that my size and gender means I am easily overpowered and dismissed. I have spent most of my life as a woman not feeling safe in my body. Patriarchy in my life means I have a constant reminder that I may have to fight for my physical safety.

I was taught as a child that courting was the holy way to find a future spouse. Courting rules taught me I was not allowed personal agency in choosing a partner and progressing that relationship in ways that felt safe to me. Instead, the authority in my life (my dad) was supposed to navigate this for me.

This is a paradigm that I rejected without understanding what I was replacing it with. I thought having feelings for someone meant I was supposed to be with them forever as a kid. Eventually, I did choose my own romantic partners, but patriarchy in my life meant I had no clue how to trust myself in my romantic relationships and self-regulate. The entire scope of consent is circumvented when you teach girls from a young age that they are not trustworthy to know when and how to share themselves.

Patriarchy in my life is any mindset or structure that threatens, minimizes, or hides parts of me because of my gender. This definition isn't specific to women. I focus here on the female experience because that's what I know, but there are so many nuanced parts of manhood that get silenced to fit patriarchal narratives.

Something that struck me about the tidal wave of #metoo was all the women who thought their harassment was normal, everyday life. We are accustomed to swallowing our discomfort and dignity to pay for our safety. But when #metoo broke, this groundswell began. If these women are standing up to their abusers and those harassing them, if these women are claiming that part of themselves we all collectively thought was gone forever, maybe we can, too. Maybe I can, too. So #metoo wasn't just saying that, yes, I've experienced harassment because of my gender, too ... but it was reclaiming our bite. It was solidarity in experience and in resolve, and that is how a movement is born.

In discussing systematic, ingrained patriarchy, my friend Heather shared:

> *My whole family has generations of molestation and rape victims. It was assumed that molestation and rape was just what guys did. My grandfather died when*

I was nine. I mentioned it to my therapist because I was really sad when he died. He spoiled me. He bought me everything I wanted, brought me to restaurants. Whatever I wanted, I got. My therapist told me I was probably lucky he died when I was nine because he was grooming me. I had no idea what that was. I broke for a couple weeks. I had no idea.

This is why I share how patriarchy has looked in my life. Because it's individual. Everyone will have a different experience, but, hopefully, seeing mine will help you remember the parts of yourself you may have left in the shadows, afraid they would make you a target, afraid you would be unsafe in your body, afraid some thing in life could make you less worthy or whole.

Heather and I also talked about how we have had to combat patriarchy in some really embodied ways. This was one of her experiences:

If you just let me do a little bit of what I want, I'm pretty happy. I just don't want to be stifled. I was stifled for so long, and then it took me over. I didn't realize how much I was susceptible to the entire patriarchy. In medic school, it would be time for me to run a scene and tell these ten big firefighters what to do. I would be like, "Hey, I'm Heather. Could you just not stand there?" One of my big things was scene management, and I thought I would be great at it. I wasn't.

The fire department goes on a lot of our medical calls, and they like to tell us what to do. Very often, they are wrong. It took a long time for me not to listen to them and realize if I continued to listen to them, my patients may die. I had to learn how to say, "No, you need to do

60

this." *They also don't want to listen to a little five-foot-five, squeaky-voiced girl. This is why I decided I needed to get stronger. If you're not going to like me, you're not going to pick things up for me, so I'm going to do it myself. Now, I can.*

I overcompensate now because I fought so hard to get my job. I applied a couple times, did okay on the test, then they said they didn't hire me because I cried on the call. I cried after the call. Since then, I've been called in a couple times, and they've been surprised at how far I've come. I tried a couple times for a couple years to get this job. My husband, Joe, walked in and got the same job with no EMS experience when I had five years, and it drove me nuts. He walked in with his charming personality and broad shoulders. I overcompensate now because I've had to prove myself for so long.

I fight patriarchy hard. I'd like to say I'm better now. Now, I'm trying to be more aware of if I'm fighting something because it's necessary or because I wanted control of my past and didn't have it. Now that I'm the one with children, I feel like I have the control. My father spends time with them, but he knows that if he screws up, I will take them away. But now, I spend all my time fighting, and it's tiring.

The negative effects of patriarchal society are fairly obvious for women, although many of us are so used to them, our identities form around them. The idea of a different dynamic where we have more choices and options can be scary because we have never been in a position where we are encouraged to set our own boundaries, make our own rules about what we do and don't want, and what is and isn't okay with us. There's more responsibility, too, because choosing patriarchy, while incredibly painful, can feel less threatening than the idea of rolling up our sleeves and getting messy creating lasting change in our lives.

It's easier to live with the mediocre at best patriarchal roles we have been handed than it is to rebuild and reform our lives when we can't see the outcome yet. So many of us have no idea who we really are. How do we know prioritizing our unknown selves and psyche is worth leaving comfort and certainty?

Releasing Internalized Patriarchy

Dismantling internalized patriarchy can be a challenging walk of faith and trust. We have to trust that this person we are becoming is what is meant for us, that what we feel is her pushing through. We have to trust that those who are meant to be in our lives will not only stay but cheer us on as they see our authentic selves emerge. If they leave, they are not meant for us. I have been amazed by how little those who really care about me are bothered by the changes that happen as I come home to myself. Instead, they celebrate my growth and achievements. We have closer relationships because we are able to be more honest with each other about what we really want in life and what we don't. This process was still terrifying. Every time I prioritized my needs over what was easy for others, I was afraid of their response. Every time I was honest about my feelings instead of smiling and nodding, I thought it might be the last deep conversation with that person (fear of abandonment, remember?). But once I took those few first steps, I realized folks were staying. Of course, some leave. Of course, I'm not for everyone. But I share a deep and liberating bond with those who know me well and keep showing up, and that makes up for the tenuous acceptance of many.

I strongly believe this is where a deep understanding of consent starts. To be able to say yes and mean it and no and mean it, we have to be in touch with our integrity and our authentic selves. There is no obligation, no getting pushed into things, no "Well, they really wanted to." If we aren't teaching our kids autonomy from the ground up, I fully believe we are priming them for abuse later in life. If they don't see us living authentically and autonomously, how can we teach them to?

Patriarchy Breakdown

One of the most worrisome issues with patriarchy is that our worth as women is defined and measured by how valuable we are to men. This creates a plethora of problems for all of us. It robs us of our intrinsic worth and autonomy as women and creates a culture of scarcity. There isn't enough here, ever. How we are supposed to feel about ourselves is dictated by ever changing individualized opinion. It sets us as women against each other, all vying for the approval of men instead of basking in always available worthiness. It shuts us down relationally, providing a very narrow and shallow space to hold all our magic. This is why we are always trying to be less. We work so hard to weigh less, to take up less space, to be quieter, less objectionable. Did you ever wonder why? In this paradigm, the comfort and pleasure of men is more important than our boundaries and integrity. To me, it feels a bit like selling my soul.

A subsequent issue that arises is the picking apart of women and femininity as if we are prototypes groomed for ideal desirability and not whole, nuanced humans. This sorting of attributes, deciding what is acceptable and what is not, is another way we are routinely reminded that society believes us to be primarily objects—a quest and a prize to be won by playing the game perfectly. So to be taken seriously or heard, we must check off every box. Of course, there are different boxes for everything we attempt, an ever-changing course we can never quite master. The game is rigged. The only way to win is to leave and collect the parts of ourselves we cast aside as unacceptable and unworthy. Some of us left our intuition behind or our silliness. Maybe we left a crazy-loud laugh or a propensity for loving "too" deeply "too" fast. Healing patriarchy means we all need to accept and own all our characteristics fully. This means our limits and our dreams, our fears and our passions.

Our Men Suffer, Too

Patriarchy hurts our men, too. It's easy to assume that patriarchy benefits men because they are in charge, but cut off from deep and multidimensional relationships, they are just as isolated. Giving men the power to determine our worth as women teaches them that we are objects, not people. It dehumanizes and objectifies us as women, which gives men a very narrow concept of who we are, what we offer, and what power we really wield. It teaches men that their worth is in being in control, taking charge, and providing amply in order to keep the things/woman/women they desire. Mothers perpetuating patriarchy often see emotional abuse of their sons as cultivating manliness, leaving boys with deep emotional wounds and avoidant attachment styles. The stress and expectation pushes many men into, at best, being emotionally distant and, at worst, performing acts of violence, especially when women don't behave as expected. They also miss out on many forms of personal growth because patriarchy dictates that we women shoulder the emotional burden and constantly make sure everyone is okay. They aren't taught emotional maturity or nurturance. To exhibit sensitivity and emotional balance deviates from the patriarchal order. This makes it almost impossible for them to break out, since every attempt at a broadening of their narrative is a direct assault on where they draw worthiness from.

Our own expectations of our men can easily enforce patriarchal narratives. Expectation of soldiering on or "manning up" during difficult times, discomfort with any displays of emotion they have, pushing them or expecting financial or other support they are not ready to extend. We also enable patriarchy by taking on their emotional loads instead of trusting that they will figure it out and gain the emotional maturity necessary to deal with their own lives.

Taking on another's pain, challenge, or trauma overwhelms us and deprives the other person of the growth opportunity. It's not our responsibility to be exhausted and overwhelmed constantly. It's not our responsibility to make sure the men in our lives are content and happy all the time, although I understand that this can often be a de-escalation tool used by women who feel threatened. The best way we can support our men is by empathizing but giving them the space and respect necessary to process what they need to emotionally. We need to remind them that their worthiness and our love for them isn't defined by how closely they follow the role society has laid out. We also need to be ready to lay down our own societal roles and step up our leadership and autonomy. When any of us misplace our worthiness, none of us win.

What Even is "Rape Culture"?

Another term that gets thrown around a lot in relation to patriarchy without clear definition or explanation is "rape culture." It can sound like a dramatic term for something that we have all lived in one way or another, but there is merit in unpacking the concept. Rape culture is a society that normalizes sexual coercion, violence, and harassment against women leading up to and including instances of rape and assault. This is the end result for both men and women living patriarchal narratives.

Men are taught to believe we women are things to be sought after and conquered and separated from the nurturing and nuanced parts of themselves, they often become violent and dangerous. Women are taught to routinely discount what we really think, really feel, and really want to gain more worth, safety, and security from men, leading to the decimation of our boundaries. So many of us have never been encouraged to dig into what we really want or don't want that we have no idea how "heck yes" feels in our bodies. If we don't know this, we can't give clear consent to anything, sexual or otherwise.

If saying yes or no doesn't feel safe to you, that's a product of living in rape culture. Yes, men need to get in touch with and own their vulnerabilities. Yes, they need to learn to see women as actual people, not shiny objects. But I'm going to be totally honest here; even the most sensitive, nurturing guy won't be able to operate within the proper boundaries of consent if we can't say yes or no and mean it.

There is a lengthy but worthwhile article by Nora Samaran called "The Opposite of Rape Culture is Nurturance Culture."[10] She makes a connection between the attachment styles we develop in adolescence and adulthood (secure, anxious-avoidant, preoccupied-avoidant, and dismissive-avoidant) and both the access we had to nurturance and secure attachments as children and specifically emotionally intelligent and nurturance modeled by men for our boys. She discusses the concept that there is no social template for male emotional development. Talking about it is often a sign of being unmanly, and those men who are nurturing had nurturing male role models in their lives.

Nurturing Men

Having the blessing of both growing up with a nurturing father and marrying a nurturing man, I see this being lived out by my brother, who is very emotionally engaged with his family, and my father-in-law, the example my husband has had to look up to. This can sound hypothetical when so often our experiences are only that of avoidant and distant men, so let me share some examples. This is not to brag but to give flesh and specifics to what nurturance can look like.

When I was little, my dad and I had a bedtime ritual that included him singing "Amazing Grace." Once, he was away at a conference before the days of cell phones. He had to use a public phone to call home, and, as it was nighttime, I requested he sing to me. I later learned there was a line of other business folk waiting for the phone, and, yes, he sang me "Amazing Grace" in the middle of a hotel lobby with a line behind him.

As I got older, Dad's chosen form of connection was waking me up early on certain Saturday mornings for breakfast outings. In my teens, I often had the "What did I do now?" question, and, yes, often, there were tensions with others in my family he wanted to discuss, but I always appreciated him taking the time and effort to sit down and talk through my perspective. Now, I see this as his way of staying connected no matter what is going on in my life. When I visit home, we often still go out to breakfast in the mornings.

My brother and his wife recently had their first child. Baby Ruby is already bringing so much joy into our lives as well as a deluge of dirty diapers. Watching my brother parent with presence is beautiful. There is nothing that isn't equally his and his wife's job in taking care of her. They are a fantastic team. On a recent visit, my brother was brushing Ruby's hair. He commented, "Of all the things I imagined enjoying as a parent, I didn't expect this to be one of them."

My relationship with my husband started with shared interest in photography, literature, and propensity for late-night chats on Yahoo Instant Messenger. Our friendship grew out of a deep mutual understanding and faith. He was the first person who I felt saw me and has held so much space for me to grow over the years. He affirmed things in me I wasn't yet ready to admit even to myself. It's almost frustrating now when I have some epiphany, and his response is, "Don't you remember me telling you this two years ago?"

I am perpetually amazed at the gauge he has on my emotional balance, particularly when we are in social situations. He checks in with me to make sure I'm okay and has no qualms about leaving when I'm ready to go. That could also be because he's always ready to go, but he also has an incredible ability to read a room and prioritize my emotional well-being.

We have an open channel of communication about our mental health and emotional needs. It's not always easy, but we work to share what we need in our relationship and where we're being challenged personally. We both struggle with depression at times, and keeping this awareness is vital.

My in-laws accepted me as part of the family long before my husband and I said, "I do." My father-in-law and I have had many great conversations. He's never afraid to ask personal questions, not because he's nosy, but because he cares deeply. He is vocal about his value and enjoyment of all his children and family. He never misses an opportunity to tell us he's proud of the good choices we are making and have made in our lives.

He has always been intimately involved in his kids' lives. When my in-laws moved, they found a box of things that belonged to my husband. Among them, we found letters to and from teachers advocating for him in his classes. My husband's dad was on the school board, coached his sports teams, and volunteered in church youth group, camp, and missions trips in which my husband participated. He even stepped down from a career in town politics in favor of being more present with his family.

I'm not saying any of these men I love are perfect and haven't experienced, participated in, or been subject to the misogynistic social expectations of masculinity. But there is a thread of nurturance and sensitivity, which can be hard to find in the world we live in. As with all things, there is always nuance and layers. There is the encouragement of nurturance and wholeness, then there is taking our self-awareness to the next level and looking for ways to leverage our personal advantages for others. We are all in different places on that journey.

I share these examples to remind us and affirm that, often, men in our lives do exhibit nurturance, and we need to celebrate and honor those moments while still enacting change. Asking them to unpack patriarchy is just as big a deal as it is for us to grow our boundaries and claim our identities.

This book is to and for women, but it is my deep belief that men need to be doing their own reclamation work. Just as we women so often have to recover parts of ourselves not deemed worthy by society, our men need to do the same. They need to check in with each other, not just with us—which can feel socially safer—and encourage each other in vulnerability and nurturance. This is how they can live into emotional intelligence and self-awareness.

In Christianity, Jesus had an iconic band of best friends, and he bonded with them through weddings and funerals by serving them meals and washing their feet, which all crossed cultural barriers. Jesus was a caretaker for his disciples and friends. He was nurturing. The book of John is an amazing perspective of this, especially. Brotherhood is just as important as sisterhood. Men need community just as much as women do. If you have ever felt uncomfortable with the groundswell of female empowerment and community happening, give some thought to why that feels hard.

If your answer is "Men need this, too" or "What about the men and boys?" you are absolutely right; men do need this, too. But male vulnerability and nurturance are not spaces we women can create past how we mother and refusing to hold mens' worthiness ransom. We can't do this for them. These are spaces men must build for themselves. We can be partners, colleagues, and encouragers, but their reclamation work is something they must lean into. The reason female empowerment is on the forefront right now is because many of us are doing scary and vulnerable work. We are building new tables out of years of trauma and intentional, excruciating healing. To achieve community and closeness, they must be ready to put in the emotional labor required.

Christian Patriarchy

In the Christian church across many denominations, patriarchy takes on many holier looking forms, which are even more damaging. One of the most blatant forms is the obsession with female purity and modesty. We talked about this in the chapter on shame. Patriarchy is the structure; shame is the catalyst. Both are equally dangerous. In the structures of patriarchal purity and modesty teachings, we as women are seen as both the weakest and the most responsible. We are not trusted to lead but still responsible for the purity of ourselves and all men. Our spiritual gifts, our testimony, and our relationship with God is viewed as secondary in importance to how we choose to cover or reveal our physical bodies.

In this paradigm, our worth is dependent on not only our physical purity, but that of everyone we come in contact with. This is ten times worse than run-of-the-mill social patriarchy. This doesn't replace social patriarchy; it adds a sanctimonious veneer. Not only is our worth misplaced, not only must we be desirable, we must not be *too* desirable. The responsibility for men and their urges, even their thoughts, is put on us as women and stands between us and our God.

This is not in every church, but the undertones of these teachings are prevalent in so many and the fallout so severe for our identities that it is imperative to discuss. Instead of a place of healing, the church can become a breeding ground for abuse and dysfunction. Where we should have protection and understanding in our families of faith, we, instead, experience more victim blaming. Is it any wonder we often cannot provide true sanctuary for those who have experienced trauma in their lives? We are doing our women and our men a disservice.

The problem for women is obvious and extensive. The problem for boys and men, however, is equally sobering. Instead of teaching them emotional intelligence, self-control, and respect, we teach them that women are responsible for their urges and desires. One in three women has been sexually harassed or assaulted, and women's self-image peaks by *age nine.*

When society starts targeting us with ads and whispers of how we aren't enough, instead of counteracting those messages, the church layers on "Oh, and you're also responsible for everyone's thoughts about your body. We care more about that than who you are, or how you are, or who you're becoming." *This is not Christian*; this is misogyny. We are so worried about sin creeping into the church, but we gloss over the long-held pervasive ideologies that were never of God in the first place.

Some look at victims of abuse and wonder why they don't leave their abusers. In the Christian community, the teachings of many evangelicals on modesty and women's roles prime women and girls for cyclical abuse.

We stay because we have been taught to believe it's our fault.

We stay because we have never been told others are responsible for how they treat us.

We stay because we have never been taught that we are allowed to have personal boundaries.

We stay because saying no or "That's not okay with me" has never been something practiced, accepted, or modeled.

We stay because we were taught to look for a partner who agrees with issues on a static checklist of theologies instead of a partner who respects our ideas, values our input, and cherishes our connection.

There are more reasons, of course, but these are the ones I have seen perpetuated in faith circles. So often, we don't arm our women and girls. Instead, we undermine their personal worthiness by chiding them about their bathing suits and skirt lengths.

We are not only made to think that parts of ourselves are undesirable and shameful, but unholy. We shear away attributes ruthlessly in an effort to become more Christ like, throwing back at God's feet gifts God has blessed us with—sensuality, rest, pleasure, emotion, intuition, connection. We *need* these God-given parts of ourselves to be whole.

My friend Jamie's formative years were heavily impacted by both dangerous religious patriarchal teaching and the immersive love and support of faith communities. This is her story:

> *I grew up in a conservative church. My parents didn't have a faith background that they ascribed to, but when they had kids, they started looking for churches. This happened to coincide with my father's mental health decline. A lot of things, like bipolar disorder, can affect you later in life, in your early thirties and forties. So he was in this period of life where his mental health was declining without really recognizing it and looking for churches.*

They found a church that had genuine people who really believed they were loving the Lord, preaching the good news, and telling the truth. It especially appealed to my dad because he was very invested in finding the "right" thing and being "right." It was also important to him because, as his mental health declined, this church validated his need to feel important as a man and escalated him as the leader and authority in our family. This was something he needed to hear as he was experiencing this mental health spiral.

Looking back, this wasn't something any of us were aware of—I was a toddler, and I don't think my mom put it together that this would only exacerbate his issues. I'm the oldest of four, so I was little, but every two years, my mom was having babies as my dad was declining. I think the church we attended would have honored and lauded her as doing the right thing and having children and raising them in the Lord. These were things she loved, and she was genuine in her seeking as was my dad, but it was this confluence of things coming together for the bad. It's like when really warm water temperatures plus a storm create a hurricane. Intense patriarchy and mental health issues come together to create this swirl of horrible.

My dad became increasingly violent. The church we attended for a very long time had leadership that told my mother she wasn't to leave him. The only way she could leave him was if he was unfaithful. He was violent, he spent all our money and stopped working, and his mental health issues were as extreme as they could be.

My mom didn't know this at the time, but while he was very violent and psychotic toward us, he was also becoming sexually abusive toward my sister and me. Everything he heard at church validated that he was allowed to do whatever he wanted because God had appointed him as the leader and authority. My mother was at her wits end seeking help, and all she got from our elders was that she was a woman who needed to obey her husband and stay with him no matter what. My mom began to suspect that this was nuts. I was seven, eight, and nine as this was building and getting worse, constantly being physically and sexually abused in my own home. When I was nine or ten, my mom began to make a plan to escape from my dad. It helped that she had friends who were speaking into her life. Many of them were people of faith who went to different churches with more well-rounded beliefs.

It also helped that around that time we had a change of leadership in our church. There's a man named Tony Terrell who played this huge role in my life and doesn't know it. He's a preacher. Ironically, he is blind, but he saw. My mom started to meet with him as the new leader of our church, and right away, he told her, "Get out." His wife also came to visit and saw what was happening. She was the first one to do that. They were the first ones to validate my mom.

So Mom made a plan to run away, and at the time, we lived in Florida. She decided to move with us to Connecticut, which resulted in my dad coming to Connecticut and kidnapping us. Mom didn't know where we were and started a police search. She found us within twenty-four hours, but he had flown us back to Florida and prepared legally for a restraining order against her. My dad, who was psychotic, had custody of us for three months without my mom being able to see us.

I experienced this as a child, and it was terrible, but now that I'm a mother, I can imagine more what my mom must have felt, knowing that a psycho had her children and what abuse he was capable of. He didn't allow anyone to see us or be near us. We were locked in a house, trapped for three months. At the time, I was ten and got really sick with ear infections. He wasn't taking care of us, just expected us to deal with it. I remember my little sister got sick and, as the oldest, I was the one cleaning it up and taking care of my younger siblings.

In the meantime, my mom would try to come get us. She was still a mother fighting for her kids. She would come, then the police would come. My parents would physically fight, then the police would come and rip them apart and take my mom away in handcuffs. It's the most traumatic thing you could imagine a child seeing and knowing. Finally, a court got involved. My mom was waiting for a court date to overturn everything my dad had set up. He is very charismatic and a good liar. He had convinced everyone in our circles that my mother was the enemy. He even told the schools to call the police if they saw her. It was this huge mess she had to undo. I can't imagine how she must have felt fighting that alone.

There was a small group of people who supported my mom, including our pastor, and a couple other churches got involved as well that had healthier views. She couldn't hold a job at this point because she kept needing to fly to Florida to fight for us legally, didn't have money to *fight for us legally, and had never worked full-time. There were some angels who stepped in and paid for things, and they didn't have to. Really extraordinary things occurred, even though so many people in church had been the enemy. I saw people of the Kingdom also being God to us. Some might say, "Oh, she must have hated church because of all the people in church who represented something terrible," and that wasn't the case for me. I saw two different versions of church. I saw this really unhealthy one that beat us down, but I also saw these other extraordinary people taking big risks to help us. We didn't have anything to offer, but they were still there. So I saw the Kingdom meeting needs and truly being the hands and feet of Jesus to a very vulnerable family.*

People see me now, and they tell a story to themselves about who I must be. "Oh, my gosh, she's a wife, she's a mom, she has a nice husband and four kids. She's on the PTA, and she teaches Sunday school. It's all roses and bunnies." So much of my life is a really stable picture, but, obviously, that doesn't tell the whole story. You'd only know if you ask good questions. I couldn't have the beauty and stability and the love I have in my life without the God I have.

I have loved reading my entire life. My mom always kept me in supply of many varied books, but I remember reading and being impressed by the stories of Gladys Aylward and Amy Carmichael specifically. Reading about their humanitarian work lit my passion for social justice and, especially, social justice with faith as its engine. Amy Carmichael founded a mission that is still thriving in India, rescuing young girls from trafficking and forced prostitution. Gladys Aylward's story also included rescuing and feeding orphans and aiding the Chinese government in the abolishment of the common practice of foot binding.

The more I think about it, the more the practice of foot binding is a striking analogy to Christian patriarchy. Starting as young as age three or four, girls' feet were bound to keep them small. This was a sign of class and beauty, although incredibly cruel and permanently disfiguring. When we refuse to question and evaluate our commonly held practices and beliefs, we risk permanently crippling our communities. We have the opportunity to remove the bindings that keep our women small and silent and our men distant and shut down. What we do with that opportunity may determine the future of our faith.

Questions to Consider for Journaling and Discussion

1. Are you comfortable enforcing and advocating for your personal boundaries and limits, even when others may not understand them? Can you share examples?

2. Have you ever felt that faith communities are more interested in how you choose to show up as a woman than your identity, calling, and gifts?

3. How did that shape your faith?

4. Do you feel responsible for others (especially men's) thoughts about you?

5. How has patriarchy affected you personally?

6. Do you know men who exhibit traits of nurturance?

7. Have you experienced Christian patriarchy?

8. How can your faith community validate your boundaries and worthiness?

5

Finding You

Dear Sister,

Thanks for sticking with me! I hope my discoveries and thoughts about shame, scarcity, and patriarchy were helpful for you. Realizing we operate out of misplaced worthiness, scarcity, shame, and patriarchal narratives, by default, can be daunting and demoralizing, but we made it.

We finally get to delve into embodied self-discovery. While this can feel like a far more positive topic, it is still messy and painful to move through. Growth is never easy. In my head, growth sounds like leveling up in a video game. In real life, growth feels like stretching past my limits. It feels like scrambling to keep up and doing everything afraid.

I might not be selling you on growth mindset here, but once we do the work of re-recording the tapes that play in our heads, we become unshakeable. Rebuilding is excruciating work, but once you've done it, you'll realize you're stronger than you ever imagined you could be.

Here's to self-discovery,
Megan

I left home when I was nineteen. I moved six hours away from my family to live near a boy I had been dating for six months. To be fair, a lot more went into my decision than puppy love and hormones. Looking back, I had found home in a person and would do anything in my power to be close to him. The fairytale adult life I had imagined didn't actually include romance before Chris. I'd listed other priorities, but truthfully couldn't imagine trusting another person that much. When I moved, I wouldn't have said it was forever. All I knew was this relationship and those I saw in Chris's family and church were some of the most honest and affirming relationships I had experienced. I was still cynical and suspicious, but hope was growing. The great thing about moving somewhere new is that people get to know you as you are right then, not as who you were as a ten-year-old or fifteen-year-old. I liked the new version of myself that I could choose to share with these new people.

While I resisted many of the rules of my childhood conservative subculture, I still formed many harmful beliefs and coping mechanisms in response to it. I believed if I had the right mix of people and things in my life with the right beliefs, I would feel happy, safe, and secure. I believed in a magic answer. Sometimes, I look back at this phase of my life and think about how many deep, probing, juicy questions I missed in search of tidy answers.

I had pictures of a lot of things in my mind that I didn't want. I didn't want to feel suppressed and limited. I didn't want to feel misunderstood. I didn't want to follow a default life template and end up in the deep end before I knew how to tread water. I didn't want to have my trust betrayed. If you had asked me at nineteen what I wanted, I couldn't have told you. Looking back, I can say that I craved autonomy and agency. I needed to know who I was past the story of my family.

I asked my friend Heather if she had anyone who confirmed her identity through her adolescence, and she said:

> *I didn't know any empowering people. Everyone I could think of was just submissive. I didn't have any heroes. I just knew it wasn't what I wanted to do. There wasn't anyone I wanted to be like, just a lot of warning signs.*

I ached for confirmation of my identity outside of what I did or didn't *do*. I wanted authentic, vulnerable connection and support in community. In faith, I wanted to see God move in my life, community, and world.

I needed to find all the parts of myself I had buried in attempts to be perfect. My voice, my assertiveness, and my limits spread out in front of me. I wondered if they could feel like mine again.

I needed to learn to expand into my full capacity for resilience, love, empathy, grief, and faith.

Heather and I discussed what advice we would have given our past selves, and she shared:

> *I tried so hard to get what I wanted on everyone else's terms, when I needed to get what I wanted on my terms. This took thirty years, and I'm still working on it. I would have just said, 'You don't have to do this. You don't have to do any of this.' I would have kept more friends.*

My journey of self-discovery and personal reclamation has been one of building enough belief and trust in who I was made to be, to look past the "right answers" I had been handed. Now, I stand here holding only big, nuanced, scary questions without a doubt that I am worthy, loved, and held. I don't feel like I've made it; in fact, I think I'm just beginning.

There are a few practical things that have greatly aided me

on my journey home to myself that I want to share. These are tools that have helped me sharpen my self-awareness, safely interact with my dark spaces, and claim my giftings and identity. They may or may not be helpful for you.

Taking Stock

The first step in my reclamation process was fully evaluating my situation. It's so helpful to watch our lives and the relational dynamics with those we love. We can gradually become aware of whether these things build us up and make us feel safe, secure, seen, and loved, or if they support our inner bully that keeps us hustling for perfect and leaves us depleted, overwhelmed, and exhausted.

There may be blaring and obvious challenges we have no clue how to tackle, or maybe we feel like things are mostly okay, but we want more meaning and connection. Nothing in our reclamation process is meant to be fast or hurried. We need to take time to silence the internal chatter and tune in to the songs our souls sing. This step is about getting to know ourselves. We can feel around the edges of our lives and observe where there is tension and where there is release and ease. Sometimes this can feel a bit like sifting through rubble. Sometimes it feels like a dance.

Heather says of this process:

> *For a long time, I mirrored what other people in my life were saying, and only recently have I considered what I really want. I tried to go to nursing school, because that's what medics do, and hated it. I'm just so tired of wiping butts. My mom says, "Nurses don't wipe that many," and I told her, "Nutritionists wipe zero." I love those odds. That's not a thing anybody I knew wanted*

to do or had done. It's like in Runaway Bride *when Maggie doesn't know how she likes her eggs. She sits down with all the different kinds in front of her to figure out what she likes. That's what I feel like my life is like.*

It's so anti-feminist, but I love Disney princesses. Rapunzel is my favorite because her attitude toward Flynn is "You can be here, but I've got stuff to do. I need to find these lanterns." Growing up, we were allowed to watch Disney movies, and they were the only things that told me I could get out. Although when I was little, it was Beauty and the Beast, *so it was like you can marry a different kind of terrible! Stockholm syndrome? No, it's totally cool. Now, they've gotten better with Elsa and Anna. My husband, Joe, was so anti Disney princess, and that's something I still really like. When we were picking names for our twins, we found Aurora as the perfect combination of us. I told him the name is scientific like the aurora borealis. He said, "I know that's a princess." She's the worst princess; she doesn't do anything but sleep. But that's our combination name. Science and princess.*

Photographer Kate Parker shared a photo of her daughter playing in a sprinkler with an ecstatic expression as part of her book, *Strong Is the New Pretty*. This image is commonly shared on social media with the quote overlay of "Remember her? She is still there inside you, waiting. Let's go get her" (author unknown). When all I can feel is noise, sometimes, I focus on who I was as a child, before I was ever ashamed of myself. I remember my creativity and how sure I was of my beliefs and what I wanted. I remember running through the fields around my parents' house, soaking up sunshine, climbing trees, picking blackberries, and playing in the mud. I remember waking up to fantastic sunrises outside my bedroom window, bursting with excitement and wonder of a new day. My path home to myself is back to this little girl.

There are so many ways to delve into self-awareness and confirmation of our identities.

I love what my friend Erika says about her self-discovery journey:

> *In college, as a woman of color, I felt like I didn't fit in socially with a lot of the other kids on campus who were kids of color. My urban experience wasn't a traditional one, so I took time to be with myself. I didn't give it a lot of forethought; I just didn't have a lot of friends from home, and my friends from school weren't vibing with me. So it started with lunch breaks then extended to weekends. I had to understand that I wasn't just a Christian or just a black woman. I had to peel that back and find my true self and say I'm not going to be solely defined by any of these labels. That was when I started signing my name "Erika Kimberly." I don't have any negative thoughts toward my dad or his last name, but I am going to be me. Who is Erika Kimberly? I have in a very old journal a sheet of paper where I wrote out words that I wanted to describe myself. I was like this is who Erika Kimberly is. She is regal, she is smart, funny, fly. I had all these words I wanted to associate myself with. I thought beyond my faith and my color. Once I was able to do that, then I was like, okay, now I can add those things back in.*

Notice & Name

After we take stock, noticing and naming our emotions follows. It sounds simple, but we live so much of our lives on autopilot without pausing or paying attention to how we really feel about things. Getting specific with naming our emotions is important. Instead of "I feel happy" or "I feel bad/sad," drilling down deeper with "I am really content today" or "Wow, I'm proud of myself for accomplishing this!" is far more revealing. It's imperative that we resist the urge to layer shame or polarized labels of good and bad over our feelings.

Feelings are directives, not decisions made or actions taken. While our feelings are sign posts to who and where we are, we are not how we feel about things. Our psyche is like a clear sky, our feelings the passing weather. Some days, weeks, months, and years are stormy. This is not good or bad; it just *is*. Uncomfortable emotions are not bad; they just are. They can be directive and informative, but there is no morality to them. We can care for ourselves by noticing and leaving ample space for our emotional weather. Sometimes journalling these changes can be helpful and telling as we get to know ourselves more intimately.

Get Curious

Once we have noticed and named our feelings, it's time to get curious about them.

"I feel frustrated. Why?"

"I feel overwhelmed. Why?"

"I feel unheard or dismissed. Why?"

"I feel invisible. Why?"

Often, we have passing happiness or connectedness but

don't know how to replicate the experience. We can then ask things like:

"What was it about this experience that was restorative for me?"

"Where do I feel at peace and grounded in my life?"

"What music brings me back to center when I start feeling tense?"

Again, there is no prescribed timeline for any of this. *Your* timeline is the right timeline. The answers to these questions gradually unlock more of the map of our subconscious. By doing this work, those of us in Christian faith affirm the confidence we have of our worth in our Elohim, Creator God. We are worthy creations, and it is worth putting time, effort, and intention into cultivating our growth.

Personal Boundaries

As we gain information from getting to know ourselves, we can begin to mindfully build what we need into our lives and weed out the things that distract and detract from our well-being. This is the foundation of implementing boundaries. I think, often, we throw around the idea of needing boundaries without doing the preliminary work necessary to know *which* boundaries are important for us. The more we practice the sequence of "Notice and Name" "Get Curious" and "Implement Personal Boundaries," the better we get at it.

Self-care is a buzzword at this point, which has almost become synonymous with "treat yourself!" This is problematic at best. Emily McDowell is an artist who recently stated in an Instagram post that self-care is really more like self-parenting. This is so important, especially for those of us who didn't have perfect parents (so all of us). The beautiful thing about self-parenting is that we have the opportunity to integrate painful childhood experiences by giving ourselves what we really need now. We have the opportunity to heal our inner child.

Starting small and implementing pleasurable self-care is always the easiest, adding in little things here and there that ground us and give us that "ahhh" exhale feeling. It can be as easy as compiling an empowering playlist or noticing that getting outside and getting in a daily five-minute walk always brightens us up or sitting outside in the mornings for devotions and rituals. Maybe a specific form of exercise feels really cathartic, and we can work that in a couple times a week. Listen to an inspiring podcast in the car. Take a bath, get coffee with a good friend. Mamas: take a mental health day away from your babies when you need it. Focus on rejuvenating and grounding *you*.

As we start to build a stronger connection with our deeper selves and inner child, we have more resources to start setting boundaries with those in our lives and start asking for what we need. I had a lot of fear and anxiety about the person I would become if I freed myself but had no concept of how much more strength, power, and connection was waiting for me to claim it.

A goal I had in therapy was to work through and dispel my fear of having kids. This was a huge anxiety trigger for me, and it seemed to be the preferred topic of casual conversation when I was a newlywed. Why people think asking about my sex life and procreation plans when I barely know them is okay, I still don't understand, but I'm just adding it to the list of social dynamics that perplex me. Rarely was "I'm not sure" or "I don't know" an acceptable answer. It was always followed by the question, which obviously has a correct answer: "Well, do you *want* them?"

I had no clue. I knew the idea was terrifying, and this decision would impact the direction of my life and family greatly no matter which road we took. More sage advice from acquaintances included "How old are you? Oh, you have time." While not wrong, I've felt this issue to be a pressing one, as there is definitely an optimal window for having kids. Every birthday past twenty-three felt like a reminder that I didn't know what I wanted, and I was running out of time for making a decision. I felt broken for not automatically wanting kids. It was yet another reason I didn't feel like a valid woman. I never felt incomplete because I didn't have children. I never felt glowy holding babies. Society (and conservative Christianity) has very specific ideas of how women should feel about motherhood that I just didn't line up with.

I reacted very strongly to the expectations that sideline so many women into lives they weren't offered alternatives for. I wanted freedom. When I realized I didn't know whether I wanted kids or not, another uncomfortable truth came to light. I didn't know what I wanted in general about most things. I had spent so long doing what made the most sense and stuffing my emotions that when I needed to tap into my intuition, I couldn't even find it.

Gradually, at the suggestion of my therapist, I began paying attention to what I wanted—for dinner, where I wanted to go, friends I wanted to see, activities I wanted to try. I made it happen. I went out of my way to do things I usually would have written off as taking too much effort and not being worth it. I began noticing a subtle change. The more I did what I wanted, the better I felt about myself, and the more personal agency and autonomy I unlocked. I gradually started prioritizing the people and things I learned were most important to me, not because I felt obligated to, but because I, 100 percent, authentically *wanted* to. Not only was this affirming, but I began to feel more comfortable gently enforcing my personal boundaries and asking for help when I needed it. Now, when someone asks me what I want, I can take a beat and give an answer most of the time.

I also read a series of books that greatly changed the way I view the relationships in my life. Brene Brown's discussion of connection being what we all need and crave was something I was surprised to see evidence of in my own life, since I have always been wary and untrusting. I became more open to connection the more I pursued what I really wanted and saw that as a driving (and acceptable) motivation. After all, if pursuing what I want is the goal, I have fulfilled that no matter what the response is from others. I realized that if they are not doing things because they are wholeheartedly excited and involved, that is their responsibility and not mine.

I am not responsible for others' responses to me. Living authentically means respecting my internal yeses and nos. The list of things I do because I *have* to include things like cooking and paying bills at this point. I am honest with the people around me about what I do and don't want and can and can't do. The result is connection because they see and know the real me, not some version of myself that I've created to be socially acceptable or "holy."

I used to have a list of approved roles and ideas of what they all looked like. Good wife, good friend, good sister, good Christian—all had different checkboxes. Throwing out those lists and just being myself with my specific boundaries was really scary but also so empowering when I realized I was enough without the lists. Just me.

Having a kid was terrifying because I knew I couldn't add good mother to that list of roles and keep it all together. I knew I would lose it. At this point, I haven't just lost it; I've given up the illusion willingly. I still don't feel incomplete without kids, but I am definitely open to inviting new life into my realm in the future. I have come to understand that there are innumerable ways to be a complete and nuanced woman, which include both craving motherhood and ambivalence toward it. Every birthday, I am excited to see what the next year brings me. I am not afraid of time or trying to hang on to some fleeting phase of life. Maybe motherhood will come to me; maybe it won't. I am happy, content, and full either way.

External Boundaries

Setting external boundaries can sound really scary and harsh when it doesn't have to be. I think internal boundaries and honesty are the hardest parts. Building up our strong yes and strong no is tough. External boundaries really are just about verbalizing it. Setting external boundaries is teaching people how to treat us, which we already do on a daily basis whether or not we put intention behind it. When we are stressed, overwhelmed, and exhausted, it sometimes feels like the only thing that will help is burning it all down, which is, of course, impractical and not usually in our best interest. It also makes us feel trapped because we don't see our way out. There are so many more options available. Often, all we need to do is make a few small changes to create some breathing room, and those direct us to where the next boundaries need to be set.

Here are some boundaries that created breathing room in my life:

- Leaving my office for lunch
- Leaving work on time, even if I didn't finish everything I felt I needed to that day
- Going to bed earlier, getting more sleep
- Plugging in my phone outside my bedroom, preventing me from waking up and going to sleep with social media
- Only saying yes to things I really want to do, no "I should," or "I want them to keep inviting me, so I'm going," or "But what if I miss out?"
- Making space in my life for those things I really want to do, no "But it's inconvenient, raining, snowing, I'll be out late, it's expensive, not what I planned"
- Being honest with those close to me about how I'm feeling, speaking my truth

- Prioritizing my integrity and limits over others' expectations of me
- Taking a break from social media
- Ruthlessly editing the social media I experience regularly by unfollowing and unsubscribing from any account that is not regularly uplifting and in line with my mental and spiritual health goals
- Following through after setting a verbal boundary, being willing to allow the fallout of things not being done if someone else doesn't come through

Changing our mindset shifts the alignment of our external relationships. People learn that we mean what we say when we are honest about our limits. We don't need to explain or justify all our decisions. "No, thank you" is all that's needed. Our language becomes more firm and sure, which minimizes uninvited feedback. We don't feel the need to chase the approval of others as much because we are okay with ourselves. This looks like confidence and feels like peace. The personal reclamation process is similar to strength training. Building muscle is slow work. The muscles must be fed enough, rested enough, and exercised repetitively with progressively heavier loads. While not everyone likes the bodybuilder's aesthetic, I think we can all agree they put in a lot of work. It takes years to attain that amount of muscle. It can also take years to develop our mental resilience and groundedness.

The journey home to ourselves can bring us through some murky and challenging places. We may go through a narrow mountain pass of anxiety disorders, the quicksand of depression, or the lonely, rocky shores of loss. We may still need to heal and integrate old traumas and wounds. There is space and time for all of it.

Processing Grief

I am coming to believe that how we move through our grief in life, no matter what we have lost, marks us. How we handle adversity in general is defining, of course, but our responses to loss, specifically, loss of loved ones, loss of relationships we wish we had or, if we are honest, feel we are owed. The perfect parent/child relationship, opportunities in life, who we could have been. Loss of childhood—growing up too fast out of necessity, loss of security, loss of trust in our communities and maybe even in God.

We all have something in life that didn't go our way, whether it's a missed opportunity or a relationship with a friend or family member that we wish was better, different, or just longer. Sometimes it's challenging to know what to do with these emotions. Often, these feelings are manifestations of grief. We need to allow ourselves to grieve. Only once we fully process this can we be present and accept what we have without trying to make it something it isn't. Maybe we have to grieve the parent/child relationship we wish we could have had before we can accept and enrich the relationship we have now. Maybe the parent isn't a safe person for us, and we need to grieve the unmet needs of our childhood self. Stuffing these feelings of frustration, longing, and anger only intensifies them. Recognize them, validate them, and maybe even integrate them as part of your personal history.

Back in 2012, my mom read a book by Ann Voskamp called *One Thousand Gifts*, and, as is her way when she really loves something, she was all in. When I got a copy for Christmas that year, I did what every good daughter would do and didn't read it. I recently came around full circle to the book again. Ann wrote the forward for Jo Saxton's book, *The Dream of You*, which was beautiful and poetic, and she also spoke at the IF Conference, and I found her inspiring. I found *One Thousand Gifts* on Hoopla (a free audio library hosted through our local library) and started listening. Ann's writing is intense and beautiful. She reads the audiobook, which adds another layer of it being very personal and real. I knew my mom had started gratefulness journaling (and became very enthusiastic about it) after she read the book, so I thought, *This book is going to be about how we are all supposed to be grateful for our lives.*

I barely got through the first two or three chapters of *One Thousand Gifts,* as it starts out detailing the profound loss Ann and her family had experienced. She'd lost a baby sister as a child, violently changing her family dynamic, and later talks about losing two nephews as an adult. I had to turn off the audiobook. Her narration was too real. She talked about watching her two-year-old nephew gradually stop breathing, and I started crying in my car, thinking about my vibrant, sunshiney nephews and nieces and how devastated I would be if that tragedy took our family. I started listening again after a few days. Ann does talk a lot about gratefulness, but it isn't the shiny story I'd expected. Instead, it's hard. It's about real, sometimes excruciating, life and handling grief.

She makes a challenging point near the beginning, that while it is so easy for those of us who identify as Christian to shut God out of our grief, rejecting the good gifts God offers only harms us further. We have the option to live a messy, excruciating life and accept God's gifts in the midst of it or just live a messy excruciating life. Jesus expressed thanks in His darkest and most painful moments. There are hundreds of bible verses about God caring for us, and Jesus exhibits grief and a whole spectrum of human emotion, but the verses can sometimes feel too familiar. Our questions in grief aren't in bible verses; our questions are hard, about the abruptness and harshness of death and inescapable loss. Our questions push back at the acceptance of a grand design and plan.

In *The Dream of You,* Jo Saxton devotes an entire chapter to

Ezekiel 37. She shares some context around Ezekiel's vision and prophecy of the valley of dry bones that I had never considered.

Jo has a full chapter on this, but her interpretation of this passage is what really spoke to me. She brought out the humanity of Ezekiel's situation—how he had been stripped of his home, his family, his friends, and his vocation through Israel's exile. She describes the exquisite grief he experienced and God patiently walking him through his trauma.

Jo goes on to describe her own losses and the slow, daily grind of living through grief. My own brushes with grief have not been so deeply personal. I have lost grandparents with whom I was close and still miss, but I have had the fortune to not yet suffer the loss of a parent, spouse, sibling, or child. I have grieved relationships and versions of people I wished I had and opportunities I felt I missed due to circumstances.

I have no advice to offer, only my presence. I have no formula, only space to process what is needed when it is time. After my grandmother died, I read *A Grief Observed* by CS Lewis. I remember being moved by the rawness of his journal after his wife passed. I appreciated the blunt honesty with which he questioned God. Something about the book being published after his own passing made it more real. He didn't write this for public consumption. There was no case he was making, only the fully authentic groping through the dark of a man sidelined by grief and loss. Even the most celebrated Christian authors question and are shaken to their very core.

So often, we all want to rush grief. Those of us in the valley want to get out, and those of us walking beside often lack the words needed. We are uncomfortable addressing and sitting with the grief. Priority is given to getting back to normal and being okay when normal and okay seem like a dream world we have awakened from to find a new post apocalyptic reality.

What I see in Ezekiel is, yes, gradual supernatural renewal but also God patiently walking through the literal valley of death with Ezekiel for as long as he needed to be there. This is our call, to show up and walk together through our traumas and our griefs. Our losses of relationship, those we love most, a projected future, how we thought our lives would go. We must give ourselves time and space to mourn the deaths of all these things. The only pathway to acceptance and renewal is through time spent in this valley of dry bones.

Healing from Trauma

Rachael Maddox is a trauma resolution educator, coach, and guide who is deeply involved in the work of helping others heal. In a podcast interview with Susana Frioni, she shared this question: "What would you do in your life if the world was a safe place for you?" I never considered myself as having experienced trauma. I have been lucky to avoid the horrors so many of my friends have experienced. I wrote off recurring nightmares, triggering experiences, and other symptoms. My body was processing past experiences as trauma.

I did acknowledge this eventually, but Rachael's question uncovered a realm of healing I hadn't considered. How many of my decisions in life were really guided by fear? What would I do and accomplish if all of me felt safe in my world? Then, the follow up, that the only way we get to that better, safe world is by taking these actions. I fully recommend working with a licensed therapist to share guidance and sign posts through healing if you have a history of trauma or you have symptoms including but not limited to: panic/anxiety attacks, depression, recurring nightmares, specific events or topics triggering anxiety attacks and emotional spiralling. Everyone's experience is unique and going to take different paths. Much of my healing process is detailed here, but it is by no means an extensive study on the topic or substitute for professional guidance.

My friend Jaime shared her history in the last chapter, and I followed up with her to talk about claiming healing and learning to thrive after trauma:

> Coming out of a traumatic childhood did bring some beautiful things but also a lot of really poor coping mechanisms. So I examine why I have the coping mechanisms I do then figure out how to undo them.

> There's a sketch comedy group called The Upright Citizens Brigade, and they have a sketch called "Stop It." A woman walks into an office facing a therapist behind a desk, and she says, "I'm having this problem where I feel like I'm being buried alive, and it fills me with anxiety." The therapist says, "I have the answer for you," and he yells, "Stop it!" And she says, "Oh, so you're saying when I start feeling this way, I should just …" And he yells again, "Yes, stop it!" So she leaves, and the next person comes in with a problem, and he does the same thing.

> The reason that's funny is we know it doesn't work. We can't just tell drug addicts, "Stop it!" We can't tell people who struggle with stealing, "Stop it." We can't tell liars, "Stop it." We can't tell people with eating disorders or depression, "Stop it." We know we should stop it, but we can't.

> I picked a bouquet of unhealthy coping mechanisms. I'm a seven on the Enneagram scale, which is the Enthusiast. For those of you who don't know what the Enneagram is, it's a personality test, and there are nine different personality types. I have three personalities, but my strongest is a seven, which means I'm an

enthusiast about everything. I'm also an enthusiast about my addictions. That's the good news.

All my chosen poor coping mechanisms had to do with destroying my body and having this tension-filled, anxiety-ridden relationship with my body. First was an eating disorder that started around the time I was ten or eleven and spanned all the way through my early twenties. I tried bulimia, I tried anorexia. I went through phases of different types. It got to a point where knowing I was going to be in a "food situation" (and that's what I called it in my head), which is anything — it's a party, it's a church potluck, it's a sleepover with your friends where there's gonna be Twizzlers — I would obsess over how much I could eat, how much I was allowed to eat, if that would make me bigger ... It was a constant assessment.

God brought so many wonderful, beautiful things into my life because I didn't know how to seek out healthy things. Help sought me out in high school. I became a part of a really beautiful group, and this is crazy because it became a cult, but it started out as something great. It was called The Weigh Down Workshop. If you google this now, it has unhealthy things associated with it and kinda became a scandal, but it taught me intuitive eating. Things like "Eat when you're hungry, and stop when you're satisfied." I had never heard that before. It was mind-blowing for me as a fifteen-year-old to walk into a space with food, eat what I was hungry for, and just stop.

In college, I became part of an eating disorder support group, which helped me acknowledge it, talk about it, and meet with other women about it. I also did a lot of reading on my own. By the time I was in my mid-twenties and started having babies, that was something I could let go of. I had these resources that helped me make peace with my body, food, and exercise. I can say I have a remarkable amount of health in this area of my life because it was such a struggle for over a decade.

So then I started biting my nails and picking my skin, and it turned into a full-blown OCD disorder, called trichotillomania. It took me years to figure out what I had, but I would literally pick my face and my skin until I was bloody. I have nails right now. I haven't bitten my nails in six weeks, and that's the longest I've ever gone in my life. I'm thirty-five. I started biting my nails when I was four. As I dealt with my eating disorder, I didn't replace it with healthy coping skills, and I still had stress. Throughout my twenties, I mutilated myself beyond measure. I really picked socially acceptable things. Eating was totally within myself, and picking myself was something I could do casually and other people don't even notice. I have scars everywhere from this. I literally one day broke down. I would find myself doing this. It was like I was in a haze and would wake up and realize I'd just made my leg bloody. This is called disassociation.

My most harrowing struggle with disassociation happened this year, actually. It's a long story, but despite my suicide plan of four years ago, my most critical mental health struggle happened at the beginning of this year. I was disassociating and picking myself and ripping my hair out. I didn't even know I was doing it. Around the time I was twenty, I started googling it to *see if it was a thing, and it is! I didn't really get official help for it. The leading experts on this have a facility in Los Angeles, and I started subscribing to their emails and participating in their webcasts. It was so helpful. Through the last couple years of my twenties, I started painting my nails because then I wouldn't bite them. Nighttime was the hardest for me, so I started a skincare routine, treating my skin kindly instead of poorly. I would set aside a half hour a day to treat my skin well before bed. I couldn't just stop the harmful thing without starting a new, good thing to take its place.*

I was still dealing with depression and disassociation. I had my most critical struggle with that when I began to disassociate almost all the time. I used to just think I was a daydreamer and had an active imagination, which I do, but people who have really severe physical and sexual trauma like I had as a kid will literally leave their body in their mind. As a kid, I thought I just had a really active imagination, which is normal. I didn't realize it at first, but I went to see my dad for the first time in over twenty years, and I was triggered.

About a month before that trip, I would literally wake up at the grocery store and not know how I got there. I would drop the kids off at school, come home, and clean the house but then wake up and not know where the kids were or how the house got clean. I couldn't stop.

This is where my social worker husband came in. I was able to explain to him. He knew about my daydreaming, but I told him that I couldn't stop. For every sixty minutes of an hour, I was out of my mind, disassociating for forty minutes. I began some really intense therapy. I literally thought I was losing my mind. This is random, but during that time, I was also on a game show. The outside of my life looked really good. But my husband was in grad school finishing the most intense part. He was basically gone for months. I was taking care of four kids by myself while having this mental health breakdown. So on the outside, if you had known me, you would have thought, Oh, my gosh, things are going so well! I lost a friendship in this time, someone who was mad at me for not spending time with them, and they had no idea I was going through any of this because they didn't ask. I'm not a closed book. It hurt that the assumption they made was that I was a bad friend, when up until that point, they knew me to be a pretty loyal person.

It's one of those things, growing and understanding ourselves and giving grace to other people. I love being the person who reaches out, but I wasn't there at the beginning of this year. I'm still doing some pretty intensive therapy. I had done a little bit earlier in my life, not as much as I should have, but this was the first time I was like, "Maybe we should meet three times a week." Because we have mental health issues in my family, and my dad's mental health issues developed later in life, I literally thought this is it; I'm losing my mind. It's really always in the back of my mind. I tell people who are close to me, "If I start acting weird, please tell me, and I'll get help. I'll get medication, whatever I need to do, right away." The havoc it wreaked in my life ... I don't want to repeat.

I also have a daily habit of exercise. I have ADHD, and I like to move. Exercise helps center me. People *think that those of us with ADHD can't focus, but that's not actually true. We are just taking in everything at the same time. I've never liked fairs or amusement parks or anything like that because it's just too much stimulation. Also, as a mom, exercise gives me thirty minutes a day that's just for me and nobody else. I take care of my skin and my body. I read and really make time for friendships. It's not just an "Oh, if I can make this work" thing; it's a need. I get together regularly with my neighbors and good friends. I started a book club. I make time for these things. Connections aren't an afterthought; they are necessities.*

One of the things that has been most helpful for me in integrating traumatic experiences is, when I am ready, revisiting my triggers in safe environments. This was one reason I started learning Brazilian Jiu Jitsu. One of my biggest triggers has always been being pinned down. I have always hated tickling and roughhousing. I have almost a response of claustrophobia to not being able to move freely. Training Krav Maga and Brazilian Jiu Jitsu put me in the position of being pinned down consensually and taught me myriad ways out of that situation. It wasn't and isn't easy, but now that I have more confidence in my ability to respond, my trigger in safe situations is greatly diminished. The process in these situations is first being in control and enacting our own boundaries then re-engaging with our triggers in ways that enable us to work through new outcomes.

I have shared my history of spiritual trauma. I do believe integration and healing are possible and following paths of personal reclamation is a great start. Many who sustain spiritual trauma feel the need to leave faith or faith communities, at least for a time. Whether they return isn't something I am personally responsible for, but I am personally responsible for helping to create faith communities that would be safe for them to come back to.

My family underwent a couple traumatic church experiences, one of which I was old enough to remember. My mom shared her perspective on both needing to take time away from community and finding her way back:

There were two or three significant wilderness experiences. We felt the hand of God with us through it each time. He always brought people into our lives to support us. The first time, we were catapulted from our home here to a six-month assignment for Mike in Connecticut that turned into three years. It took all those years for the healing to take place. We just wanted to go sit in the back pew then leave. We wanted to lick our wounds and hide. But God brought us into the most amazing oasis of our lives. We were involved in a family-oriented church that had our values, and they gave us a lot of strength. It was so wonderful that it was really hard to come home. God really ministered to us in an amazing way there.

The next one was not so easy. We didn't really believe in home churching, but we were in a situation that relationally went very sour and became dangerous for us to stay in. We left, but we didn't feel comfortable going to another church. We didn't want to carry a relational mess to another community. We thought it was going to be short-term since we were looking for reconciliation and closure, and that never came. We home churched for about eleven years. We went to a church our other daughter, Bridget, was loosely affiliated with for a while, then we found the church we attend now. You asked how it was reintegrating into community, and it was hard.

It wasn't the fear of the situation repeating; it was more a feeling that community is messy. I wasn't ready to be open to that yet. Just sitting through a service was hard sometimes. There were days I went straight to the car after worship because I was done. When I see someone do that now, I get it. I mean they may also just have to go somewhere, but there are people who do not linger, and they may have a really good reason. The most amazing thing was that the pastor and one of the women who did administrative work would thank us for our presence, just for showing up. That ministered to me. They couldn't know what it meant to us at that time to just have our presence valued. Gradually, I started working with the children's ministry, and I started getting to know the families. Then D group (discipleship group) was the real catalyst for community.

My friend Kelly experienced a church community that encouraged her growth in faith but then couldn't hold space for her emerging gifts. She shares:

I grew up not even having a Bible in my house and having a family who would not talk about God. I went from never going to church to becoming radically saved about ten years ago. I became heavily involved in women's ministry in the church then parted ways with the church, which is where I am now. It's been a radical journey from the get go. I think I was very hungry for God. There are a lot of things that have happened in my life since I met Jesus that would not have happened otherwise. I experienced a lot of healing through the church. Then I came to a point where I felt like I was being suffocated, and I really couldn't grow anymore in that space, so I stepped away and went in a different direction. I didn't step away from God, but I did need to step away from the church. At one time, I really needed to be poured into. I needed to release a lot of stuff. It happened at the right time in my life for me to go through some healing and accept things that happened to me. But after you get poured into, you need to release that on the world. Sometimes, if you stay in the same place, you're pigeonholed and put into a box. You're subject to what everyone else wants for you. I came to a place where I couldn't share what I had learned.

Mental Health & Wellness

Mental health disorders can be a huge factor in our personal growth and development. I've shared my own struggles of depression and anxiety here, but many folks struggle with bipolar disorder, dissociative disorder, multiple personality disorder, and more. Seeking professional help is always a good idea; however, my personal strain of depression and anxiety has responded best to mindfulness practices, setting boundaries, and surrounding myself with supportive people. Mental health disorders don't present the same for everyone. My depression is triggered when I overextend myself and burn out. My anxiety is triggered when my internal boundaries are low, and my inner empath tries to manage everyone's emotions. Others may have different triggers and presentations.

Get to know yourself, and get the help you need. The first time I remember struggling with depression, I was a teenager. I didn't have any resources to combat it with, and it didn't really break until I was nineteen. Even then, I didn't have a good handle on managing it until I spent time developing self-care rituals and getting to know myself better through therapy. I explain depression and anxiety to those who don't experience them as those relatives you really don't associate with or talk to, but you can never predict when they are going to pop up in town. I find not personally identifying with it to be helpful (eg: I am not depressed; I experience depression). Realizing this isn't part of me helps me re-center and reclaim myself from it.

Depression can be passed down genetically, and both my maternal and paternal grandmothers as well as my mother have struggled with it, so it's no great surprise the depression monster visits me, too. The sneaky thing about the anxiety and depression one-two punch is that after dealing with anxiety attacks, the apathy that accompanies depression feels like a welcome reprieve. Everyone has a different threshold and marker for depression, but my personal warning sign is if talking myself into getting out of bed every morning for a week or more is a herculean effort. When I pick up the phone and listen to a disgruntled client while thinking, *You have no idea how much effort it took me to even show up today*, it's time to get some help.

My friend Erika shares:

> *I went through a really bad depression, and as I came out, the word "fearless" came to me. Depression has its own grief cycle, and there's a lot that had to die for me to be where I am today. What people see and enjoy is a byproduct of a lot of dark things. From that, I decided to be fearless. I decided what was making me sick and sad was not living my truth. It was not being the creative woman God has created me to be. Not being the thoughtful writer God has created me to be. So now I say I've made the world I want to live in. I also learned not to force myself into spaces that make me feel small or like I have to act small. The world I'm choosing to live in or see, I'm operating in my own space, and I'm doing it every day. Things that don't fit within that gotta go.*

*I said goodbye to a lot of great people who just weren't
great for right now, where God and I are going.*

Rituals

Rituals and routines, especially in the morning, have been
so helpful in growing my internal boundaries. If I start out my
day from a place of groundedness, it's easier for me to find it
again when chaos ensues. This has included, at various points,
everything from devotional study, to yoga, getting outside,
pulling affirmation cards, lighting candles, and eating breakfast.
Prompt journalling is something I move to if I'm having a
particularly challenging time getting grounded. There are all
kinds of prompts you can use. My favorites are from Neghar
Fonooni, who is a coach, speaker, and writer. The prompts are:

- Physical check-in (How am I feeling in my body?)
- Emotional check-in (How am I feeling emotionally/
  spiritually?)
- What actions can I take today that help me improve how
  I'm feeling?
- What intention do I want to set for today?
- What intention/mindset do I need to release today?
- What 3-5 things am I grateful for?

These are the prompts I have utilized regularly as part of
my morning rituals. Sometimes, even the physical and emotional
check-in questions are challenging, forcing me to get mindful
about how I'm feeling, putting me in touch with my body. It's
also a short process unless you want to write a lot. I have a
deck of affirmation cards from Erin Brown that I love. I pull
a card almost every morning as a reminder/intention for the
day. My depression kicks into high gear when we fall back an

hour and generally during the winter, so I have a light therapy lamp that supplements sunlight. When it is warm and light out early enough, I go outside. Having even ten minutes dedicated to putting myself into the mindset I want to carry throughout my day is incredibly helpful. The more we practice grounding, tuning in to that still, small voice and finding peace in stillness, the more we will be able to access that in chaos. I have a few repeatable scriptures that have become mantras/life verses. My favorite is "Be still and know that I am God" (Psalm 46:10, NKJV).

Music

Another tool I have utilized is creating empowering playlists. During depressive episodes, I muster the energy to first make coffee, eat breakfast, and do my morning rituals before getting in my car and turning on the playlist. By the time I get to work, I can go in. I used to feel this was a little hokey or silly, honestly, until I started reading *The Women Who Run with Wolves* by Clarissa Pinkola Estes PhD. Dr. Pinkola Estes is a Jungian analyst, and *The Women Who Run with Wolves* is a psychoanalysis of folk and fairytales about women from across the globe. One of the first stories in the book is the story of La Loba: wolf woman who gathers the bones of deceased wolves and sings over them to bring them back to life—literally re-membering them with her song. When I read this, something clicked. The playlists and music aren't silly, they aren't random, they are what re-members and brings those lost parts of me back to life. I listen to the same playlists and albums over and over sometimes for months on end, depending on what I'm re-membering. The main playlist that is particularly affirming is comprised of all female artists. There's something sacred about hearing another woman sing power over me that I have yet to claim. You can find my playlist on Spotify, titled *La Loba* (warning: some songs are explicit). On really tough days, I have popped in headphones at work on lunch and taken myself *out* of that stressful situation, allowing myself to get grounded and come back in with a clear headspace. I also find driving a great time to listen to audiobooks, podcasts, and sermons, depending on what I need that day.

Ultimately, we all have to build our own toolkits for self-care. What works for me may not work for others. Learning self-parenting and inner boundaries is an exercise in getting to know ourselves and our needs better. It's about tuning in to our inner frequency. Only once we get grounded and claim who we really are can we offer any semblance of sacred space to others.

Questions to Consider for Journaling and Discussion

1. Have you ever practiced taking stock, noticing and naming your emotions, getting curious about them then setting appropriate boundaries?

2. What boundaries have you set or do you feel called to set with others?

3. What boundaries have you set or do you feel called to set with yourself?

4. What activities and spaces in your life give that feeling of exhale and release?

5. Where do you experience cyclical low points—regular times of day, week, month, or year—that are hardest?

6. How can you hold extra grace for yourself during those times and build up your self-care?

7. What verses, poems, or mantras speak strength, comfort, and courage to you?

8. How have you moved through grief in your life?

6

Finding Sisterhood

Dear Sister,

If you know me at all, you know I'm all about sisterhood. You may have heard me talk or post about how Malala Yousafzai was inspired to be a journalist by watching America Ferrara play one in *Ugly Betty*. This tiny snapshot shows how we all need all our gifts. As Marian Wright Edelman says, "We can't be what we can't see."

My idea of sisterhood used to be tied up in the stories society and church told me about women. Once I started experiencing the power of authentic women coming together and sharing their gifts, my eyes were opened to a whole new world.

This is the world I want us all to share. We've talked about self-discovery and self-actualization because community amplifies what we exude. If we don't do the work of self-awareness and understanding, we won't be able to tap into the full power of sisterhood and community.

Sisterhood is one of those things that sounds awesome but often feels impractical when we start evaluating our schedules and priorities. I hope this chapter helps you break down barriers to participating in community and inspires you to find your people.

So glad you're here,
Megan

I didn't have many girlfriends growing up. There were three childhood friends I counted as "best" friends, two of which I'm loosely in contact with today, but we aren't integrated in each other's lives. Through my teens, I had some online friendships that served their purpose but always left me wondering, if push came to shove, would these people actually show up for me, or are we "close" because it's easy to type into a void? The answer was yes to both, as I eventually married one of my good online friends, and one of my very best girlfriends began as an online friendship. There were also those who fell off as life got more demanding and real for us all.

This was a painful process for me at the time, but I can look back on the span of those friendships and feel profound gratitude for their place in my story. I started watching *Friends* long after it was over, when my parents got dialup. (If you're too young to remember what dialup is, Google is your friend!) I would let an episode load for over an hour to spend twenty minutes watching it. Originally, this was part of my social project of figuring out what "normal" (hah!) people watched and to find some common ground as a secluded homeschool girl. It became one of my favorite TV shows, but I also remember having this longing for that close-knit friendship dynamic.

I was jealous of friendship far more than romance in books or TV shows. More recently, Chris and I watched *Girl Meets World*, and some of those old feelings resurfaced. I remembered how alone I felt at the age of the girls on that show. When it came time to pick bridesmaids for my wedding, I could not find four women to match the number of my husband's groomsmen. My sister was my matron of honor, and two friends from my new Connecticut life were bridesmaids. I tried to fill that last spot, but it wasn't meant to be. I was uncomfortable with how the choosing of a wedding party put a spotlight on my lack of girlfriends, but I laughed it off as confirmation that I was one of the guys. I just didn't identify with a lot of the "girly" stuff women supposedly cared about. The truth was, outside of the two friends who were in my wedding party, I was isolated.

Loneliness is a rising epidemic in our society across men and women alike. A study published in August of 2017 stated that loneliness and social isolation could be a bigger threat to public health than other well-known risks. In *So lonely I could die*, Julianne Holt-Lunstad presents data from multiple research studies questioning the role social isolation has on our mortality rates. The studies concluded that social isolation, loneliness, and living alone all have a similar, significant effect on premature death, which are equal to or greater than other well-known risk factors.

My friend Jamie experienced this when she became a mom and was launched into a new life phase. She shares:

> *I have always been big on friendship, community, and connection. I'm an extrovert. I watch my seven-year-old daughter, and we are so similar. I watch her enter a situation, and within four minutes, not only does she have a new friend on the playground or at church, but they're literally holding hands and skipping. If that was acceptable for me to do, I totally would.*
>
> *I had great friendships through high school and middle school. When I became a stay-at-home mom, it was a big change for me. I'm an extrovert, but now I'm always home, and I'm an adventurer who is playing this role of a homebody. I'm doing two things that are outside of my strengths. In addition, I'm a stay-at-home mom where there's winter six months of the year. It compounds the isolation. When you're a mom, it's easy to just let things*

go by, and I didn't realize at first how much it was devastating my friendships.

I became a mom very young, so no one else had kids. I wasn't in the places that my friends were. Over the first year, I felt so isolated and couldn't figure out why. I also moved, so friendships were in transition anyway. Moving and motherhood happened at the same time. Then no one I knew was in this phase of life, so I had to make all these new connections around the phase of life I was in. I got really intentional about it five or six years ago.

I had a period of losing friendships for natural reasons and had some falling outs. I had very few solid, vulnerable relationships in my life. When those left because of moving or falling out, I realized, Wait, I'm down to no one! I became so unhealthy. Four years ago, I came the closest in my life that I've ever come to suicide.

I was so isolated and so unhealthy. It was something I had struggled with before, but it was the most real at that point. I saw how dark and desperate I was. I also have an amazing husband who helped me in this. I have this crazy life, and God sent me a mental health professional to be my husband. God was like, "You're gonna need someone special, someone who knows the terminology. Someone who knows a lot of therapists."

I became ruthless about choosing myself and choosing to be completely authentic in any new relationships from then on out. I needed to know if people were staying or

going because everyone that's in the boat needs to be
rowing.

Our lack of ability to find deep and meaningful connection with others is actually killing us. Past generations had pressing reasons to stay in close contact with each other through multi-generational living arrangements and interdependent communities. Now that we have different dynamics, we need to be more intentional about community and relational connection to stay healthy.

Female friendship can be particularly challenging for several reasons.

Hustle

Most women are already busier and more emotionally overextended than we would like to be. Be it work, school, or family, taking time and energy away from the demands of our lives to put toward relationships that can feel uncomfortable and vulnerable is challenging. My friendship with my first bridesmaid started because I locked myself out of my apartment, and she lived downstairs. If I could have been by myself in my apartment at that point in time, I would have been. I knew her in passing, but almost forced time together is what kick started a friendship that I cherish to this day. My other bridesmaid was my roommate, who has since moved away, but when we get together, we pick up right where we left off. Both of those relationships started out of proximity, and they were my only close female friends at that stage of my life. There's nothing wrong with close friends formed through proximity, of course, but it is important to pay attention to the amount of intention and energy we put into finding and keeping up our female friendships. In her book *Frientimacy*, Shasta Nelson makes a great point about prioritizing friendship. She goes back to the old analogy of how to fit sand, gravel, and rocks into a container. We all know the big rocks have to go first to fit the gravel and sand around them; otherwise, it will never all fit. Shasta makes the point that friendship and connection is one of the big rocks. She references a 2006 study conducted by James Coen, PhD, a psychology professor and director of the Virginia Affective Neuroscience Laboratory at the University of Virginia. He tested the cortisol levels of sixteen women through MRI scans. Researchers compared their responses to an electric shock, which elicits a similar physical response to the stress we feel, either while holding their partner's hand, while holding a stranger's hand, or undergoing the shock alone. Results showed that a third of their cortisol levels lit up in the brain when they were comforted by a close companion. Shasta illustrates that friendship actually buffers our stress in life, making us healthier when we share close relational connections. Friendship isn't a luxury; it's a basic necessity.

Depending on Where We Are in Our Journey Home to Ourselves, Other Women Can Seem Intimidating or Even Threatening

Patriarchal society teaches us that other women are the enemy, our competition. This is a lie. Not only are other women not our competition, we are strongest together. Through all of my most transformative experiences as a woman, I have been surrounded by sisterhood. Christian sisterhood, sisterhood of heart. When we women show up with one intention and bare our souls, it is powerful and healing. We also find what we look for. If we are finding shallow and unfulfilling relationships, maybe it's time we adjust our focus and look deeper. Accepting our worthiness allows us to hold all the space for other women to bring their unique magic to the table. We can celebrate them and be filled with awe at their presence without an ounce of jealousy or comparison.

We Often Try to Silence in other Women those Traits We Have yet to Accept in Ourselves

We are judgemental of the woman who luxuriates in her sensuality because we are scared of our own. We are uncomfortable with the bluntness of the woman who knows all her boundaries because we cannot yet prioritize our integrity and needs over what has always been and what makes others in our life comfortable. We squirm when we hear the woman deeply in touch with her intuition talk about listening to her gut instincts because we have been writing off ours for years. Bringing awareness to this discomfort and getting curious about it is hard but necessary work. We need each other to remember. We are given to each other as a way to become whole. For a long time, I minimized the role that femininity played in my life, and I find it no wonder that during that period, my female friendships were few and far between. Now, women are some of my favorite people. We are so diverse and have such varied skills and experiences, spanning a wealth of knowledge and history. I can honestly say I *love* women. I love the boss babes running their businesses and lives. I love the boss moms running their families. I love the students of school and the students of life. I love the doers and the thinkers. I love the stories we all share of our families, our histories, our communities, and our lives. I celebrate the divine feminine in all of us. This is the community waiting for us on the other side of judgements and fears, too busy and too burnt out. It holds a wealth of love and empathy, balm for a strung-out, isolated life.

We Think Our Friends Have to Be Permanent

I used to have a very strenuous (for me) evaluation process when considering new friends. Are they likely to stick around? Will they unwittingly embarrass me or betray my confidences? I used to take months evaluating and watching people who probably barely knew I existed to see if they exhibited the necessary qualities. I obviously had trust issues, but what I've learned is that change is inevitable, and sometimes people are in our lives for a season, and that's a good thing. Parting ways at some point doesn't mean the time we've shared with them was any less special. Walking any part of life with another is an honor. Now, I allow my friendships more breathing room and flow. I reach out and contribute as much as feels authentic to me, and when there's a connection, it's exciting and inspiring. I don't have a lifetime of expectations attached to that connection anymore. If it lasts for a month, a year, or more, it's totally okay. Investing in a friendship is never a waste as long as I am reaching out authentically.

We Have Been Hurt by Women and/or Teachings on and from Christian Women

The week before I was co-opted into attending my first women's retreat with my church group (thanks to my mother-in-law), I sat in my therapist's office close to a panic attack. Most of the teaching I had received up to that point for Christian women was limiting, and I had done so much work to heal from Christian patriarchy, I wasn't sure if I could deal with hearing it preached again. I was afraid of having to fill a specific role. I was afraid of getting triggered by teaching from which I was still healing wounds. I went with trepidation, and it was one of the most wonderful experiences that planted the seeds of my

117

passion for women and women's ministry. I got to know the ladies from my church on another level and really hear what was on their hearts. I learned that we aren't all that different. We all share so many struggles and challenges. I was also troubled by the lack of attendance from women my age. There were a wealth of matriarchs praying over their families and communities and so many women my age missing out on them and their wisdom. These women have done it; they have beat this level of the game of life already! It's easy to think the older generations don't get our struggles, don't understand what we are going through, but this is a lie of disconnection. Sure, some older people are stuck in limiting mindsets, but so many of them are still growing and changing and have so much life to share with us. We wonder where female leadership is in our lives, and if we lack it, it's on us to seek these women out.

It's true that there is damaging Christian teaching when it comes to women, but we cannot let this be an excuse to isolate ourselves from our sisterhood. My go-to coping mechanism in life has always been of the burn-it-down, cut-them-out variety. I have isolated myself. I have decided I didn't need girlfriends, or sisterhood, or anyone. My answer to rejection was "I didn't need or want you anyway." Eventually, it took almost nothing for me to pick up my marbles and go home. This felt safer than the threat of conflict or advocating for myself.

Isolation feels murky and thick, like dark, suffocating fog. We feel like we are the only ones getting beat up by life. When we reach out, even just a little, we realize we are shoulder to shoulder with other women, living the same, messy life. When we light a match, we realize there are millions of us in the same place fighting the same battles, and we find our sisters in arms. If we don't reach out and share our needs, there is no way for the sisterhood to know what they are. We Christian women cannot be frustrated that women's ministries don't relate to us when we are not vocal about what we need to see. If we don't see what we need, maybe that's our call to build it. If I am not showing up, how can I be seen? If I am not looking for Christian female leadership in my life, I will not find it.

We Don't Know Where to Start

It can be really hard to find people we connect with naturally. As I let my guard down and started putting more effort into connection and relationship, friendships started forming. It wasn't a deep dive from day one with all my close friends, and there are several different groups that serve different purposes with different kinds of connection. I have one group of five to six women, which is large for this introvert. We were all coworkers in the past, and I love the interest and care that we all have for each other's lives.

Their group texts are the only ones I stay in voluntarily. I love that I never give a crap what I'm wearing when we get together or worry what they will think of me. (They tell me.) No other group has made me laugh as much as they do or gotten me through tougher times than they have. If you're in the beginning stages of looking for female friendships, start paying closer attention to the women already in your life. Find ways to celebrate them. You'll know who belongs before very long, and it may not always be the person you first thought. Once upon a time, there was an extroverted woman at my church who, at first, just naturally rubbed up against all my triggers and fears. As an introvert, she seemed like a social energy vampire, and I needed to conserve my sweet energy juices. However, as we got to know each other better, we became good friends. She started a book club, which has been a wonderful experience, with a great group of local women. We sit, we talk, we drink wine and eat crackers with cream cheese and jelly, and deep dive into what is on our hearts. It's a beautiful space that grew out of her desire for meaningful connection and community, and I am honored to be a part of it. We so often feel lost, disconnected, vulnerable, and overwhelmed, not realizing the warmth, depth, and support available to us. We are fighting the same battles, dealing with similar struggles and challenges. We have so much wisdom, grace, and support to share, and it is *meaningful* and needed.

Feeling Our Gifts are Not Needed and Denying Our Own Need for Connection and Support

We have stores of untapped energy, power, and support that many of us have never even been aware of. I have also felt for so long that to admit need was to admit weakness and lack of worthiness.

In *Rising Strong*, Brene Brown asks, "How can we be truly comfortable and generous in the face of someone's need when we are repelled by our own? Wholeheartedness is as much about receiving as it is about giving."[11] She then goes on to discuss how, in her life, helping was praised and lauded and states, "Helping was the most value I brought to a relationship ... Offering help is courageous and compassionate, but so is asking for help."[12] This chapter hit me hard. I had never considered that my belief system, that I was a better person for being a helping person, cast judgement on those I was helping. How could I really offer help and meet needs if I was unable to ask for and accept what I need? *Of course*, I am keeping everyone at arm's length if I can't even admit that I need their presence in my life. *Of course*, I cannot be authentically seen, heard, and supported if I refuse to participate in that vulnerable exchange and *accept* support.

I am learning that asking for what I need is a skill to be developed just like learning a positive work ethic. I have to actively work to ask for and accept help. This may be one of the most revolutionary experiences of participating in therapy, that initial understanding and breakdown of realizing that we don't have this, and we need help. It happens in faith, too. When we take on a walk of faith, we agree that we need divine help and intervention to save us from this epidemic of sin. So often, though, we want that to be the last time we need or have to ask for help. We're "saved" now. We're good, right? This isn't the faith or walk modeled by Jesus. When He was human, He allowed Himself to be ministered to, to share community, to rest, and He even asked His disciples to "keep watch" with Him as He prayed in His final hours. Jesus practiced asking for help and support, and He was divine. How much more do we need each other?

In our interview, Jaime described the first time she had help as a mom so poignantly:

> I don't have a lot of family or natural support in my life. My husband's family lives far away. My brothers and sisters all live far away, and my mom still works full-time and has a busy life. I don't have that "Hey, Mom, I'm having a bad day. Can you come babysit" option.

> I remember the first time I had help vividly. I had three children in three years. I had an infant, a one-year-old, and a new three-year-old. I went to a group called MOPS (Mothers of Preschoolers). I had never been; someone recommended it to me. We met every week, and it was a ministry of a church to provide nurturance to mothers who were constantly nurturing. They would provide childcare for two hours and let you have a conversation by yourself with a mom.

> I thought I was okay in motherhood. I hadn't stopped nursing or being pregnant in three and a half years. My

body was recovering. I was constantly caring for my kids. My husband traveled, and I was by myself with them all the time. I had become so self-reliant just keeping everything going. At the same time, this big other thing in my life was reversing generational trauma. Everyone who came before me in my life grew up in trauma. My mom grew up in trauma, my dad grew up in trauma, I grew up in trauma, and for the first generation, I'm trying to parent normalcy, something I don't know and have never seen. I'm like a duck, looking smooth on the top and furiously paddling underneath just to stay afloat. I came to MOPS that day, and they handed me a hot cup of coffee, and they took my kids and babysat them. It was the first time in motherhood anyone had ever helped me or watched my kids during the day for me. Any doctor's appointment I had for myself, I took all three kids. Any dentist appointment, all three kids. Any appointments for any of the kids, all three kids. I took all three kids everywhere I went, every hour of the day and never had a break. Rather than responding with "Party time! I get to sit with moms!" I was so overwhelmed with gratitude that I sat there and ugly cried for two straight hours sobbing and heaving.

I hadn't had a cup of coffee in one sitting in four years. I held this hot cup of coffee and stared at it, like, What is going on? *I was like,* Oh no, these are supposed to be my new friends, and I'm pretty sure they don't want to be my friends anymore! *They just kept handing me tissues. I had no idea what it meant to me to have help because I had never had it. There's so much I didn't know and so many ways I wasn't looking at my life to find the resources that were there. There were resources there; I just didn't have the eyes to see them at the time.*

The very hardest part of creating vibrant and fulfilling community is admitting we need it. I'm writing this book for others, yes, because I believe my journey may be relatable, may be helpful. I am also writing this book for myself. I'm writing it because I need this community. I need you in my community. I need your story, your perspective, your laugh and energy. Our circle is not complete until we all are there. I believe you need this authentic and vulnerable space, but the space needs you, too. There is infinite wealth in this sisterhood. I have personally been supported and blessed so much by the older and more mature women who have so much life experience and wisdom to offer. I have been inspired and encouraged by women my own age and younger who have so much energy and vigor to share. We all have needs to be met as well as something to offer.

I love how Jaime started growing intentional community and support. She shared with me:

> *I set out to really intentionally build a community that could support me. I would purposely "date" people. It got that intense.*

> *I set up alarms on my phone to text certain people once a week with certain messages. I thought,* Regardless if this person wants to be friends with me, I'm going to call them and text them once a week at least. *I had a calendar and strategized spending time at least once a month with different people. I had seven people that I really wanted to get to know better, and I pursued them. I've told a couple of them this now, and they said, "Oh, that year? Yeah, that's the year we just got closer. It's funny how we just got closer."*

Then I showed them my calendar and said. "Oh no, I chased you."

During the time I was trying to date my friends, I also recognized that for so many women who are mothers, we rarely have uninterrupted conversations. You're talking, but you're constantly meeting needs. There was one specific friend in my life who I felt I was being called to, and she was an introvert. I'm friends with a lot of introverts, and it can be exhausting usually being the initiator, but I got this idea to reach out to her and start a book club. The same day, she messaged me and said, "We should start a book club!" She started the book club, then she moved away, so now it's my book club.

I had this really diverse group of women in my life, and I recognized the power in that. I wanted a reason for us all to connect. I invited women who I knew would show up and take it seriously, who were spiritually driven and connected people. It was a hand picking of people who I wanted to grow with and learn from. This particular year, we are choosing books by women of color, and I want to hear those voices. I tend to like non-fiction, so most of the books have been non-fiction. Honestly, I would have joined anyone's book club, but no one invited me, so I decided to be the inviter, and now people are showing up!

When I bought my house five years ago, God put us in a cul de sac that's literally a circle of cool people. They're mostly retired, but I have this beautiful group of old ladies I play cards with every couple of weeks. In the wintertime when it snows, they come over to my house for chili. My geographical location has become a place *of sisterhood. I put a lot of intention into developing friendships in our neighborhood. I plan the block parties, and everyone knows that when it snows, after they dig out, to come to our house for soup and board games. It's really amazing.*

Being a mom is also such an asset to meeting people you wouldn't normally befriend since your kids want to play together. One of my very best friends, I never would have been friends with her. We are not alike at all. But I love her and have learned so much about what it means to be a mom from her. We do have similar upbringings and levels of family support. I admire her so much. Now, we're at a place where we can laugh about our differences.

As my community and sisterhood has grown, I have begun to make a conscious effort to ensure that my social media and informational intake isn't just from people with stories and lives like mine. I have the ability to curate who I listen to and what I see in my social media feeds. If my understanding of sisterhood and faith only speaks to women like me, it is incomplete and exclusionary. In *Half the Church*, Carolyn Custis James makes the point that God's vision for women includes not only the middle-class married women with children but the single, the single parents, those in lower economic brackets, and especially women still trapped in extreme patriarchy and violence. If our gospel doesn't include and speak to them and the horrors they experience daily, we're still missing something. Furthermore, our circle of sisterhood is not complete without their gifts. We need the perspectives and experiences of women outside our bubbles and comfort zones.

My friend Erika founded a women's ministry called To Be Praised, and she shares:

One of the core principles for To Be Praised is to address women as women, not women as who they are to someone else. Who are you as an individual? Who did God create you to be? I always use Eve as my benchmark, and I use Mary. The Bible is full of women who were strong and were forerunners in their generation. I look at Esther, and, yeah, Esther became queen, but she had to check the king and be like, "Hey, don't kill my people, okay?" and in that moment, I think Esther was Esther, because she had to literally go up against the thought of someone who could have killed her instantly. I think one of the biggest pitfalls we still perpetuate today is this idea that a woman is less of a woman if she is not attached to someone else. I'm anti that. I've always been anti that. I think by being thirty-three and unmarried, I've been able to speak to people and show women that you can be independent and still love God. There's this misconception of what it means to be a woman when you're not in a relationship with someone else. I'd say that's one of the biggest ones. After that, there's this whole kid thing, and we use that as a gatekeeper.

"So when you havin' kids? How many kids do you want? Well, when you have kids…" And it's like, no, I can serve now, I can lead now, I can teach a class now. I am still valuable. How many times has Jesus shown us in scripture? Mary and Martha were hosting a bunch of men in their house. So that's a couple of the pitfalls I think we get tripped up on. I just try to do my due diligence and see women as women, not as labels.

If the story or perspective that a sister shares makes us uncomfortable or brings up inner conflict, we need to use our reclamation tools and do some examining of ourselves. Part of releasing patriarchy as women is releasing comparison. It's easy to say there is room for all of us and we all have needed voices and stories, but sometimes, it's hard to deal with the emotions that come up when we watch other women succeeding where we long to.

These feelings aren't about them. They are about our stories and an invitation to more closely examine our path and boundaries. Often, those feelings can be directive, showing us where we are not living authentically yet or showing us where we need new self-care rituals. Sometimes, it shows us desires we have been shutting down or a new direction to pursue in life. Sometimes, we just need to remember the realities and commitments that our sister's accomplishment required and take a long, hard look at whether that's something we would actually want to commit to instead of being jealous of her mountaintop.

Those of us with biological sisters know they can be our closest allies and best friends, or we may go through seasons of being less connected. We can also have the most poignant and challenging throw downs. We would do well to remember this. In *Frientimacy*, Shasta Nelson discusses varying friendship circles, reminding her readers that best friend status or "frientimacy" isn't achieved in every friendship, and that's okay. Frientimacy takes a long time to forge and is reserved for those relationships that have withstood years of connection and history. I've pointed out reasons we are often disconnected in this chapter, but my intention is not that we all become best friends today, but that we start evaluating our relational sisterhood with more intentionality and mutual respect.

There is a wealth of connection available to us through our sisters, but this is not to say that we all have to commit to the sisterhood the same way we would commit and drop everything for a best friend. That would be intensely overwhelming (especially for us introverts) and likely violate many personal boundaries across the board. I do think there is a level of personal commitment necessary to invoke sisterhood. Squad mates in war may not be best friends, but we all know they hold a special bond forged in life or death scenarios. We must live by a similar code. This isn't about being besties; this is about taking care of our sisters in arms. No woman should be left behind.

Here is my code of sisterhood, my commitment to all of you.

I will fight for your safety, autonomy, and voice. I will defend your calling, and I will rally behind your ministry and purpose. I will trust God's anointing and leading in your life. When you are wounded, I will help you find healing and rest. I will celebrate your gifts and your magic as you continue growing into the person you are designed to be. I will do everything in my power to be a light on your journey home to yourself. I will hold space for your messy, imperfect, vulnerable, and authentic self. I see you.

Will you join me?

Questions to Consider for Journaling and Discussion

1. How have your closest female friendships developed?

2. What needs can the sisterhood meet in your life?

3. How have you experienced relational isolation and loneliness?

4. How do you choose to show up in the lives of your sisterhood and cultivate connection?

5. In your busy schedule, how do you prioritize sisterhood?

6. What are the big rocks, gravel, and sand in your life?

7

Finding Kingdom Focus

Dear Sister,

One of the most wonderful and terrifying things about community is that it provides us accountability. This chapter is especially for my sisters in faith. I believe we have a sacred responsibility to remember where we first pledge allegiance. So often, we get mired in the prejudices and systems of the world we live in. It's so easy to pledge our allegiance to comfort, security, or status first.

I believe in unity of faith and purpose in my soul, but we often don't examine what unity asks of us. Unity asks us to consider who we are leaving out. Unity asks us to evaluate how our beliefs serve our greater community. Unity asks us to laugh with those who laugh and mourn with those who mourn. Unity asks us to openly lament the trauma caused by systems of oppression we have participated in. It asks us to lament the harm caused by both ourselves and our ancestors.

This might not be an easy chapter, but it's a necessary one. If we are going to build community, we must be willing to face our collective shadow side. I hope this chapter helps you take the next step toward inclusive community—whatever that means for you.

In peace, love, and unity,
Megan

I have always been passionate about humanitarian and social causes and known them to be actively tied to my faith. My mom gave me many biographies of amazing women as I mentioned in "Releasing Patriarchy," Amy Carmichael, Gladys Aylward, Harriet Tubman to name a few. My social education on the topic of race relations, however, only started a few years ago, when I believed racism was a problem of the past. I had an incredibly patient friend in a biracial marriage who shared vulnerably with me. Her and her husband's experiences opened my mind ever so slightly. I acknowledged that there were still terrible, very bad, no-good racists among us and went on with my life.

Then, Trayvon Martin was murdered and ushered in a succession of gut-wrenching examples of how systems of racism are still alive and well. It finally hit home that this wasn't a handful of hateful people. It was a series of hateful systems built into the fabric of our world.

As I began to educate myself, a growing sense of responsibility welled up inside me. I saw in example after example from history and current day that the powerful systems that allow me to live my life without a second thought to the color of my skin often hand out violence, pain, and trauma to others. Just like the fact that I'm female is always a factor I consider—going somewhere alone, taking a walk in the dark, pumping gas, parking in a parking garage—many people of color make similar considerations for a different reason.

I realized that just like I have participated in patriarchal systems, because that's the landscape I was born into, I have also participated in oppressive racialized systems. I can't deny the reality of racial history without denying the generational trauma my ancestors inflicted on (especially black and indigenous) people of color.

Erika shares:

> There are systems in our country that have dictated how smaller communities operate. It's hard for us to reverse what is happening in the church without reversing what's happening in our community, which then follows reversing what's happening in our country at large. I think a lot of it is systemic. I grew up in the 80s, which was right after a really important time in this country when black people were given the right to be seen as equals but also the freedom to operate as equals. My dad was born in the fifties. What was happening to black people in this country in the fifties? So now, as an academic, as a scholar and researcher, I get that. As a younger person, it was just blowing my mind every day that life was this wild. You can enter one space and feel like no one and enter another and feel like, "Wow, I'm Beyoncé." I think the time that I was born in shapes how I view inequity. It is highly systemic.

My crises of faith have never come from if I believe in God or not. They have come from whether I can hold space for all the horrific acts carried out in the name of my God and not lose hope.

Isn't it ironic that to profess Christianity, we must acknowledge and deal with our sin, but some of the people most resistant to acknowledging the roles they and their ancestors have played in creating global trauma are Christians? Shouldn't we be the first to echo King David and say our sin is ever before us? Shouldn't we be at the front lines of repentance and restoration?

The Problem with White Jesus

If you're not with me yet, if you're thinking this is a political scam, let me ask you this: How many representations of Jesus have you seen in TV, art, and in primarily white churches that show Him as a person of color? What is His hair usually like? Is it dark or blonde? Is the texture coarse, or does He always magically have beach waves? Are His eyes blue or brown? Now think about His heritage. Where was He born in the world? What was His lineage? Does it line up with the most traditional picture of Jesus we have, or have we literally made Him in *our* image?

If we have taken Jesus, the figurehead of our faith, and made him white, I think this, in and of itself, is a reason to talk about race.

Why do we need to make Jesus white? If it's for artistic expression, then again, why is white Jesus with beach waves and, as Barbara Brown Taylor notes in *An Altar in the World*, no body hair, more artistically and aesthetically pleasing to us than a realistic interpretation? Why do primarily white actors play Jesus in biblical dramatizations? Why do we need to make Jesus look like us to relate to Him? If we whitewash the most important person in our faith stories so we can relate better to Him, what does this tell us about our capacity to hold empathy and relationship with our brothers and sisters of color?

Racism isn't a slur, insult, or even simply a name for holding prejudice. Racism, like patriarchy, is a system, which, no matter our intentions, we all have been born into, and many of us still drastically benefit from. I'm not saying we don't have hard lives. I'm not saying we don't carry trauma, haven't been bullied, worked multiple jobs to make ends meet, or experienced other forms of discrimination (hello, being female!). One of the first things I learned in therapy is that others' experiences, which may seem more drastic, don't cancel out or minimize my own. If I—my body, mind, and soul—processed an experience traumatically, I need to have the tools to heal from that experience, even if it seems others have dealt with worse.

Discussion of the system and the negative power dynamic of racism does not minimize or cancel out our efforts or negative experiences in life. It only means the deck is still stacked against others. When we write off the stories of our brothers and sisters of color because their experiences show the world in a different, less flattering light, those of us who profess Christian faith center ourselves in their stories and put ourselves above the Kingdom we have pledged allegiance to.

Just as a man can never experience the challenges and disadvantages of being a woman, so those of us who are white cannot speak to the experiences our brothers and sisters of color face at the hands of a system that has handed us security and status. To achieve unity, we must decenter ourselves. I'm not sharing these things to pass shame or judgement. I'm sharing because these issues impact us all, and how we choose to apply our faith directly impacts our brothers, sisters, and neighbors. This isn't strictly a social issue being fought by social justice warriors, whom we can easily discount and turn off. If we choose to turn it off, if we choose to look away, to pretend people aren't hurting, that mothers aren't losing sons, and children aren't losing fathers, and mothers aren't dying for lack of appropriate medical care, we are choosing the side of the oppressors. If we choose to close our hearts and homes to those who have lost theirs in war-torn lands, we choose the side of the oppressors. If we allow the officials that we've elected to separate families as they run for their lives and hold their children in warehouses, we share the responsibility of the oppressors. When we prioritize our comfort, ease, and security over lives being lost and our own creeds of faith, we join the oppressors.

I am not responsible for the creation of these systems I was born into. I am, however, responsible for what I do with all the resources I am handed in life. I will give an account as to whether I used them wisely, to spread peace, love, and faithfulness or to make myself more comfortable and fortify my security. We Christians so often think of our resources from a financial standpoint. We often pride ourselves on giving monetarily, sponsoring mission trips and missionaries and humanitarian aid projects.

Sometimes it's easier to give across the globe. It's easier to send a mission team for a short-term project than to make sure the regular ministries we offer are accessible and helpful to low-income families and for those whom English may not be a primary language. It's easy to give a one-time donation. It's hard to change our ways of life and thought patterns.

Kingdom Centered Vs. Self-Centered

Throughout His entire ministry, Jesus worked to instill a kingdom mindset in His disciples and followers. Time and time again, they are confused and bewildered by things that seem clear as day to us now, in hindsight. Yet, we often fall into the same traps and habits they did, quarrelling about who is the greatest, finding ways to make life and faith about us and discredit those who aren't like us, those who may disagree.

Kingdom focus and mindset can be one of the most challenging concepts to enact as a Christian. From Eden, we have fallen prey to the temptation of self-centering our lives. The temptations of humanity were nuanced but are so often reduced to a glib story about a woman eating some fruit. Not only were we tricked into lusting after connection, relationship, and wisdom we were already offered, the temptation of "being as God" was a manipulation of perspective, offering humanity the illusion of control and having a centered role—a deciding role, a powerful role.

It's an instinct we are born with. We center our experiences because they are the most vivid to us, so they seem the most pressing, the most ... legitimate. This can be an unfortunate source of division among us as brothers and sisters in faith. Instead of working as co-laborers and bearing one another's burdens, we fight about who has the correct interpretation and perspectives of life and faith, when, in fact, all our experiences are both diverse and legitimate. Our experience of life, though, whatever it may be, is not the point. The Kingdom of God is the point, and we have a sacred responsibility to keep that as our priority.

A large number of similar people all feeling they should be centered in life is dangerous. If we can look around us in our lives and find regular representation—in society, media, and faith—of people who look and think like we do, if we feel we are the default and therefore automatically justified, we need to be especially wary of our mindset in this area. When we make decisions that favor others similar to us, it sets up unhealthy and sinful dynamics in our lives, churches, and governments. It is vital that we learn to detach and decenter ourselves from our experiences. We must both hold space and grace for our journeys and realize that our journey is not the only journey, even if that's what we see around us. If we are to love our neighbors as ourselves, we must learn to accept others' narratives and journeys to be just as valid as our own. Sometimes, this may cause discomfort. Their journey may not center us or people like us in the way we are used to.

When we live as though we are the stars and center of life without taking consideration of others' stories, we almost always cause harm to the outliers. The temptation here is to protect our status, what we feel we have built and are owed instead of listening to those telling us their uncomfortable and sometimes deeply painful truths. Our first instinct is often to justify ourselves and center ourselves in their story instead of listening to them, seeing them, and loving them. We need to repent of centering ourselves. Good intentions are wonderful, but unless they are followed up with bold actions of love, affirmation, and collaboration, they are empty. We need to learn to not only accept those with diverse stories but champion and amplify them. Jesus sought out those who lived on the fringes, unaccepted by society and religion. If we are living in mainstream and enjoying all the luxuries of it, we are no better than the rich, young ruler. Living by the letter of the law, we have missed the Kingdom.

I recently had the honor of engaging in a discussion holding quite a bit of tension. In the past, I have always shied away from tension or disagreement as they are uncomfortable. However, I realized, sitting in this group of women respectfully and passionately sharing their hearts, if we want growth in our communities and ourselves, we must welcome challenge.

Invoking Grace in Hard Conversations

From watching the culture wars currently raging, I have come to realize that to engage meaningfully in disagreement and emotionally charged discussions, we need an upgrade to our relational toolboxes. The difficult part of this is that these are life skills, things we must practice daily and live out of. I have already discussed most of these in depth, but I want to highlight *why* they are so vital when it comes to having courageous conversations.

When our *worthiness* is misplaced, we often feel threatened by those with different experiences and perspectives. We are easily tempted to center ourselves in their stories and experiences when our sense of worthiness comes from being right, good, or chasing perfection. When our worthiness (no matter what) is in our creation and origin story and the redemptive work of Jesus, we are able to listen to others' stories and experiences without needing to justify ourselves, our lives, or our roles. We can hold space for their journeys no matter what light that might cast on our own. We can be open to growth, broadening our perspectives, repentance, and asking forgiveness readily without shame when our worthiness is aligned.

Waking up to the effects of *patriarchy* in our lives is often a first step in being able to understand how power dynamics can wreak havoc on society. I know I have been able to relate to stories others have told me of experiencing discrimination because of what I have experienced as a woman. I know what it's like to regularly feel vulnerable because I'm female. I know what it feels like to always be aware of who is in an elevator with me or walking behind me. I have doubted my voice, calling, and faith because of my gender and what I've been told God says about it. It's not a far leap for me, with this understanding, to see that male/female is not the only damaging power dynamic at play in our society and, yes, in our churches.

When we armour up to avoid *shame* and vulnerability, we misplace our worthiness and cannot share the meaningful connections we are meant to. Fighting shame with vulnerability enables us to hold courageous conversations with those who have been harmed by discrimination and acts of hate.

We cannot hold open, loving discussion and be ruled by *scarcity*. Scarcity sees everyone as an enemy, looking to take what we have, instead of family. Imagine if we saw the many displaced peoples of the world looking for sanctuary and home as brothers and sisters in faith who we just haven't had the honor of meeting yet instead of potential security threats and additional mouths to feed. Our scarcity has the ability to blind us to the needs of those around us. When we spend all our time worrying about having and being enough, we miss divine encounters through the most vulnerable and marginalized.

Paying attention to when and why we feel defensive is a fantastic tool for self-evaluation. We can use our reclamation tools to dig further into our mindset. Taking stock of why we are feeling defensive is always an important first step, followed by noticing and naming the more specific emotions. Do we feel hurt? Guilty? Shamed? Challenged? When we get curious about this, our defensive emotions can become instructive. We avoid so much harm and conflict by learning to process these things ourselves instead of lashing out at those who are often already wounded.

There is room for *all* of us at this table. We all need space to be heard and seen. If we are excluding anyone from community, we are doing it wrong. This chapter isn't only about racial differences and divides, but those are some of our most obvious ones. If we find it easy to ignore or write off these challenges, it is directive of our priorities. If the color of our skin isn't an ever present factor we take into consideration, we need to take a step back and listen to those who live that reality before discounting it.

My friend Erika weighed in on the challenges of being a woman of color in the church:

> *I grew up going to a predominantly white church and always felt like I was on the defense. This is stuff I don't usually talk about, so you're getting the deep thoughts. I remember being a kid, feeling like I was on the defense based on things people were saying, jokes people made, all highly racially charged. Again, as a kid you don't feel powerful enough or knowledgeable enough to quantify it. I hadn't taken a critical race theory class where I could combat that from the angle I would now.*

> *Being called to those spaces, I believe God brings us there for refinement. When I look back on it, it was necessary for me to go through that because I needed to know up front that we are always contending for our*

faith, and sometimes that comes from people who also have faith. We have this misconception that it's always coming from people on the outside, and people of faith really need to do a better job of understanding people of faith. If we start there, everything else will fall into line.

The spaces I shape are really imprinted by my life experiences. I'm very intentional with To Be Praised as a ministry and business model to have something that reflects my life. I have friends from all walks of life and all ages and backgrounds. I could only link up with writers, but sometimes I want to talk to a photographer or someone who's awesome with event planning. I know what it's like to feel like you're always on the defense. I know what it's like to feel like there's not room for you to be authentically yourself. That was really challenging to me as a young person and when I was in college. Again, in college, I went to a predominantly white church, and I was like, "Where's my mom right now?" It wasn't like I needed a mother figure; I just needed a black woman in this space who gets this. I try to be very intentional about including people from all over my life because I don't want people to have that feeling that I had. If ever someone does have that feeling at one of my events, I know I've stepped away from my true self.

The Sixty-Second History of Organized Christianity and Human Rights

Even though racism flies in the face of the basis of our faith, it has undergirded the organization of Christian religion for hundreds of years. Churches are memorialized alongside slave trading posts and holding cells. A well-known one is Elmina

Castle in Ghana. According to reports from International Justice Mission, a church is located directly above one of the holding cells, and it is said that the congregation was often asked to sing louder to drown out the cries of those suffering below. George Whitfield, a founder of evangelical faith, was not only a slaveholder but brought slaves into the newly formed colony of Georgia, where slavery wasn't yet legal, for cheap labor to build his orphanage.

The church's history does not show Christians unified on the forefront of doing our Messiah's work—binding up the broken hearted, proclaiming freedom to the captives and release from darkness for the prisoners (Isaiah 61:1, NKJV). Instead, we hang back, afraid of the ramifications bold actions could entail. Denominational splits happened through abolition and civil rights eras based on interpretation of scripture and to what degree the church felt racial equity was justified in faith.

Historically, we find ways to justify our social structures biblically, especially when they benefit us. For many years, the church sanctioned slavery. The church didn't condemn slavery until well after abolition movements gained traction and still sanctioned segregation. Now, the church doesn't condone or implement segregation but also rarely takes any stance socially, always looking to preserve comfort and stability, or should I say its patrons? Spain and England taught American colonizers not only grisly warfare tactics but how to use religion to control and manipulate indigenous populations. While this may not be what we want to associate with our religious history, we must be able to acknowledge our collective shadow side. If our ancestors could convince themselves the people crying for help—interrupting their worship services—were less than human and their agony was acceptable, how can we say we would have been abolitionists if we are not fighting for equity today?

Our faith calls us to a global, diverse sisterhood. There is no way for us to carry this out and be self-centered or defensive.

We must not only accept and help our sisters from all walks and backgrounds to heal; we need to celebrate them, encourage them, and support their callings and ministries with our time, energy, influence, and finances. We must lament our history and seek ways to actively bring about restoration. We can't ask those who have histories of generational trauma to join us in unity if we haven't proved we have learned from our ancestors' mistakes.

Embodied Collaboration

I love Erika's thoughts on this. She says:

> *I think it's important to reach across the aisle. What you decided to do was courageous because even the first time we came to talk, you were just intentional and curious. I respect that a lot because when people step across any aisle, when they say, "Oh, I want to get to know you," they come with this preset; there's a block there. Literally, it's just walking across the aisle, walking across the room, driving across town. There's so much power in that. Also, just understanding that it's exhausting for "the other," whomever that is. Let's take the example of someone who is disabled. How exhausting is it for them to come to your space for years and years? I don't believe people who are in any type of smaller group should always do the heavy lifting. I look for ways to check myself. Say, "Okay, Erika, there are ways in which you're privileged. So what am I doing? Where am I getting out of my comfort zone to cross an aisle and say to someone else, "Hey, I see you. What's up?" I think that's huge.*

Two words I always tell people are: make room. The whole idea of make—it's a verb, it's an action, you have to do it. I get so tired of people saying, "Oh, you know, we sent a flyer." That's not making room. Asking me to speak is making room.

Churches are filled with people, so even having cultural celebrations is great. We do a lot of eating, and the church I go to is so cultural and multifaceted. I love it. I feel like our potlucks are how Acts 2 would have been. If everyone heard in their own language, that means they were all representing different spaces, so you would have someone from Nepal bringing rice and someone from Jamaica cooking curry chicken, and my mom cooking macaroni and cheese. Even something like that. We talk about having a seat at the table, and food does a lot for people. I would just like us to engage with one another's culture and not be afraid of it. We should do it with love and curiosity and take it from there.

For me, that's what's complicated. By taking the action step, we're showing we don't have fear. On the flip side, maybe someone is thinking, Oh, are they afraid of us? Are they afraid of our church building? Are they afraid that we clap? *There are all these fears people have, and just being present dispels a lot of that.*

Celebrating our sisters' gifts leads to building amazing new spaces through collaboration. I want to use whatever platform I hold to magnify the powerful stories that so often go untold and unheard.

My friend Jaime describes this as "minding the gap":

In New York City, there's a space between the subway platform and the subway. It's a six-inch gap. On the subway and the platform on both sides, it says "Mind the gap." If you don't, you're going to lose a leg. It's a small gap, but it's critical if you miss it. It has become a metaphor. We have this black and white picture blown up on our wall at home that says, "Mind the gap" as a reminder to us of all the places in our lives where there are gaps. They may be small places, but they are critical, and we can't fail to make that small jump to enhance community, enhance justice, enhance connection, and flourishing in our lives and in the lives of others.

Some of the gaps that come to mind for me are generational, especially in church spaces. We underestimate the role generational gaps are playing. It doesn't have to be a big deal, but we still have to be aware and account for it. Especially in churches, gender is a major one. We are not comprehending the gap and the way it needs to be crossed. I think personalities is another, having grace and space for our friends with different strengths and types of personalities. Also, single parents, working parents, and single people in general. I was raised by a hard-working single mother, so this topic is dear to me. There are two people who my husband and I pray for and text regularly to check in and support them. Same thing with widows. This is what the church is supposed to be doing. It's something we do as a bonus but not a primary focus, and it's supposed to be the point. Mind that gap!

There are also racial gaps. Let's not forget it. Just because we are both white girls doesn't mean we don't know that this is a massive problem. It's a gap we need to walk with such ginger, tender awareness in faith and honesty. As white people, we need to simmer down and listen. Something we've mistakenly identified as what God wants from us and what "ministry" is as fixing and helping, when, really, it's about showing up and loving. Just being there and journeying with people is the important part. Fixing isn't even in the top ten. The dynamics that plague our entire country plague our churches, too.

This is one of those concepts that we can all agree on, but it can feel cumbersome to enact in our day-to-day lives. I want to share an example of collaboration that really struck me.

Jen Hatmaker is a Christian author and speaker. She recently interviewed Latasha Morrison on episode four of her "For the Love of Women Who Built It" podcast series. In the interview, Latasha talks about how she attended the first IF Gathering in 2013. IF is a wonderful community of vibrant women focused on female discipleship. However, at that first gathering, Tasha noticed an intense lack of diversity. She was already living out her calling of being a bridge builder in her own community by creating a space to openly discuss and work through racial tensions and divides. God laid on her heart a vision for global sisterhood. One of Tasha's friends knew Jennie Allen, the founder of IF, and encouraged Tasha to meet with her and share her concerns. Here comes the key part—Jennie not only met with Tasha and her friends and listened to them without defensiveness, but she encouraged Tasha's mission and helped her mobilize more discussion groups and create a replicable program. Then the following year at the IF Gathering, Jennie invited and encouraged Tasha to speak about her mission to a crowd of over 3000 mostly white women in person and thousands more through global live streaming. She quoted Jennie on the podcast as telling her, "This needs to come from a person of color. You have to lead this. You have to lead us in this. This is not something for me to lead." Tasha was hesitant and afraid, especially as her program was new, but this was the birth of Be the Bridge on an international scale. Tasha has now been recognized as one of *Ebony Magazine's* "Power 100" in 2017 for her vital community work and continues to champion bridge building and racial healing, which are so needed. Her book *Be the Bridge* was birthed in October of 2019 and should be your next read. This is collaboration and mutual female leadership.

There are a few key factors here I want to highlight. In no way am I crediting Jennie with Latasha's gifting, mission, or success. I do want to talk about her role here, though, because, while we need to uncover and develop our own giftings, we also need to learn this vital work of collaboration.

First, Jennie took time and energy out of her own ministry and life to sit with Tasha and her friends. She showed up to this conversation.

> *If we look around our circles and don't see diversity of all kinds, we need to start looking for places to show up for our sisters outside our current comfort zones and bubbles.*

Second, Jennie came with an open heart. She didn't come to defend her ministry, herself, or her platform; she came in humility to listen and learn.

> *When we are approached, or we hear about inequality and injustice, we need to be able to invoke humility and openness in that space. How can we leverage our own platforms and ministries for a whole and healed faith community? Doing our own personal work in worthiness and reclamation will enable us to listen to*

*others' experiences and ministries without attempting to
make those narratives about us in any way.*

Third, Jennie spoke into and encouraged Tasha's ministry. She built relationships and continued walking with Tasha and her friends in community and healing. She supported her without taking anything over, continuing to take the position of a follower. She kept showing up. She didn't just show up once and decide she had fulfilled an obligation; she kept participating in community.

> *What ministries in sisterhood are we supporting
> and encouraging? How do we participate in those
> communities on a regular basis?*

Fourth, and maybe most important and striking, *after* doing all of this and building rapport and community, Jennie leveraged her own platform and influence to amplify Tasha's message and ministry.

> *How can we amplify the ministries and messages of our
> global sisterhood to those we influence?*

Fifth and lastly, Jennie recognized this was not her call to share. She didn't go to IF and just talk about Latasha's ministry or co-opt her message and take credit; she recognized Tasha's gifting and calling in this space and stepped aside for her.

> *We need to be aware in our zeal and excitement of what
> our call and ministry is, and what is a sister's. Just
> because we connect with it doesn't make it ours. Who can
> we share our platform with? Who can we step aside for?*

Republican Jesus

I'm learning all this right along with you. I grew up in Western New York, which, while beautiful, isn't exactly the diversity capital of America. My family didn't talk about race much. I read a few young adult biographies of people of color through homeschooling—Harriet Tubman, Booker T. Washington, Amos Fortune, and, of course, George Washington Carver. I'm still not sure why it stopped there, why we didn't move on to Martin Luther King Jr., Malcolm X, bell hooks, Angela Davis, Alice Walker, Maya Angelou.

While race wasn't discussed much, politics were consistently. I grew up during the Bush/Clinton and then Bush/Gore elections and gathered that Jesus personally endorsed George W. Bush and probably also listened to Rush Limbaugh at least occasionally. Republican Jesus is full of inconsistencies (as would be Democrat Jesus, to be fair). But Republican Jesus was the filter through which I understood race after abolition. I mostly felt like I didn't *need* to understand it because everyone was free now and just needed to get their act together. Sure, there were still some no-good, very bad racist people, but even most of them couldn't be faulted too much because they "grew up in a different time."

Republican Jesus told me I didn't need to get to know my neighbor, that my struggling brother and sister in faith just needed to pull themselves together. But I think the most harmful belief of all was the belief that I didn't need to understand race as a white person because it really didn't affect me.

I never had to decide whether to put an Americanized "white" version of my name on my résumé to raise the chances of getting a call.

My parents didn't sit me down and have a conversation before I started driving about how to interact safely with law enforcement were I to get pulled over or if I was in a car with someone who got pulled over.

I trusted that if I were in an unsafe situation, I could call the police, and I would be taken seriously as a victim and protected.

Last summer, I was driving back from a plant sale with a friend, and we decided to stop for iced coffee. She offered to pay, so I left my wallet with my keys attached in my car and locked it. In the middle of a sleepy Connecticut town, we called the police department, and they dispatched an officer to let me back into my car. I spent the forty minutes or so it took him to arrive thinking about how this might not be a safe situation for someone who wasn't me. I had locked my wallet with my ID in the car as well, but he opened it for us without even questioning whose car it was.

Privileges & Advantages

For some reason, the term "privilege" raises some of our blood pressures. But the definition of privilege is just "A special right, advantage, or immunity granted or available only to a particular person or group."[13] Isn't it ironic this is the only setting in which we don't want to be special? Maybe because then we know that makes us responsible, too. Some of us are so used to our privileges, we have no idea what life could be like for us if we didn't have them. Recently, there was a list that went around social media of twenty-plus things women do to try to stay safe. We passed it around and commented our number, how many of them we do regularly. Men rarely did even one regularly, but most of them don't go around thinking, *Wow, this wouldn't be a safe situation for the women I know*. This is an example of privilege.

Last year, my husband, Chris, went on an unconventional job interview. It's hard to know what you're really in for from only electronic and phone contact until you show up. His interviewers invited him to get into the car with them and drive to a coffee shop for the interview. He was annoyed by the unprofessionalism, the loudness of the coffee shop, the fact that the company was sketchy (surprise, surprise), and the fact that the car he had to get into was tiny and uncomfortable. The first thing I said after he told me this story was, "I would never get into the car with someone I just met; that's how you get abducted." In the words of one of my MMA instructors, "If you let them move you, you're probably dead." He was uncomfortable in this situation and frustrated that his time was wasted. For me, or any other woman, that same situation would set off warnings of being seriously unsafe.

Privilege has many layers. There are gender, economic status, skin color, sexual orientation, and more. The point here isn't to be ashamed of our privileges but to recognize them. To realize that, sadly, being or feeling safe in our world is a privilege, and that's a sign something is really wrong.

Claiming Unity

Educating ourselves on racial healing is vital to carrying out the great commission. We are not only to share community with people who look like us. Racialized society is perpetuated by those of us who continually prioritize our comfort and security over equity. Let me share some examples:

We white Christians often miss the opportunity to worship with our brothers and sisters of color. Our efforts to reconcile often are limited to outreach, attempts to bring diversity into the spaces we have created instead of seeking out congregations that are already diverse and learning from them. The Bible is not silent on topics of cultural blending. The early church had many clashes due to differences in culture and custom. Paul, however, did not preach a gospel of segregation. That could have seemed an easy fix—let the Jews and Gentiles worship separately how they are accustomed and avoid further conflict. But that was not his answer. Instead, Paul gave direction to actively change the structure of the early church to make sure the needs of the widows and the poor from all backgrounds were being met. In fact, the solution included making sure those handling and dividing the money were representative of those in need. This is something I have yet to hear a sermon on. There is a huge difference in encouraging racial reconciliation by expecting all those who aren't like us to assimilate and get with our program and looking for ways to learn from and celebrate their cultures instead.

Many calls of unity from predominantly white Christian groups put the burden of forgiveness on (especially black and indigenous) people of color while we continue to participate in social constructs that cause them harm. Forgiveness follows lament and repentance. If we have not openly acknowledged the trauma and harm we and our ancestors have caused, we can't achieve unity. For an in-depth study of this, read *Be the Bridge* by Latasha Morrison.

Stepping into global community is twofold. First, there's the learning, finding empathy, study, and self-examination. Then we have to start doing things. We have to get uncomfortable and set new priorities. We have to be okay driving somewhere new, not knowing what the parking will be like, and not being centered.

The practice of Christianity and the call are often divergent. Jesus's ministry was intensely and uncomfortably counter cultural; however, we regularly perpetuate cultural practices that feed power dynamics, securing our status but ultimately bringing harm to our brothers and sisters in faith.

This is one way in which the ideal of having a "colorblind" society is harmful. Not acknowledging color is not a marker of reconciliation. It actually means we are actively ignoring rich cultural history as well as very real oppression. Being colorblind assumes everyone is like us, which turns off our ability to learn from those who are different and immobilizes our empathy. We cannot respect others fully and encourage them to become the people they were created to be and assume they are just like us, and if they got with our program and tried as hard as we do, they would be successful.

Individualism and Community

Living in an individualistic society has pros and cons. You would think a highly individualized society would lead to being known more and having a greater sense of autonomy all around; however, that is not always the case. Instead, we become more isolated and lonely. It's almost impossible to view our lives through the lens of individualism and not take hard topics personally. It's almost impossible not to get defensive because the hard topic, instead of being about a system, culture, society, or power dynamic, is now about you specifically, or me specifically.

We hold the miracle of individual relationship with God through Jesus in our lives every day, but in our personal faith and highly individualistic society, we often miss the very big and real effects that shape the landscape our stories play out on. When (especially black & indigenous) people of color point out injustice and inequity, it is not usually pointing to us specifically; it is pointing out vast differences in the landscapes we are handed. Shaking our heads and telling them we just don't see it tells them not only are we oblivious to their pain, but we don't care enough to listen. We actively value our own ease, comfort, and security over who they are and the lives they live. When we make their commentary on power structures and inequity personal instead of corporate, we make their pain about us. We want to hear that we are okay. We want them to know we aren't racist instead of focusing on fixing the unequal systems. We want our worthiness validated.

I am not advocating for any easy answers. I believe the solutions to these challenges are multifaceted. Some of them *are* individual. We individually need to become self-aware and start taking a harder look at how integrated our communities are and fasting and praying over ways to grow greater unity. We can purposely start attending more diverse events and making personal connections with more brothers and sisters of color. We can individually hold our political representatives accountable and encourage them to find ways to make our landscape more equal, even if this means we have to, in some way, financially support their efforts. We can have hard conversations with family and friends about the evolving racial landscape instead of just shifting uncomfortably and changing the subject when it comes up. We can spend time and effort educating ourselves about the history of people of color, especially black and indigenous people who were most affected by colonization, as well as discovering and celebrating black, indigenous, and other authors and artists of color we may not be as familiar with. We can ask our church leadership how our community is moving toward racial reconciliation, and if it's not a high priority, brainstorm raising awareness and conversation in that space. This is not easy work, but it is critical work.

Baby Steps

As I have worked to educate myself in racial healing, a few themes have emerged. I am not an expert by any means. There is a wealth of information available for self-education on these topics. Instead of seeing racial disunity as a topic to carefully avoid, maybe it's time to dig into the nuance of it. Let your discomfort instruct you in ways you might be called to step up and do better.

The first thing I have done to expand my frame of reference about racial tensions is to:

Seek Out Diversity in Our Media and Social Media

If we can scroll through Instagram, Facebook, and Twitter and see only faces and stories that reflect ours, we need to actively reach out and follow those from different walks and backgrounds.

Actively Seek Our Own Education

People of color who are the victims of systemic trauma are not here to teach us to do better or educate us. Some choose this work and build spaces of healing and community. This work is grueling, and just as we women build spaces of healing from our trauma, so do educators with histories of racial trauma. The very least we can do is financially support their projects and not expect any of this education to be free. Some of them also create healing spaces specifically for others who share their history and give us the ability to donate toward scholarships. This is a fantastic opportunity to not only support the educator but build up the community.

There are a multitude of resources available online and in our libraries. Often, our cursory history education does not even skim the surface of what black, indigenous, and other people of color endured. The wealth of information available through our libraries and online speaks to the depth and complexities of the topic.

We Must Amplify the Messages and Ministries of Our Brothers and Sisters of Color

Co-laboring means sharing and abdicating the stage and platform so their messages can be heard. This may not feel like faith work, but if we are to live our faith and fly its colors, we must push past our comfort zones. We cannot fulfill the great commission and stay comfortable and secure. Our ministries, organizations, and churches must be structured with a deep understanding of the global church—the church God sees—not just our corner of the world. We are not there until we are all there. If our ministries only edify and uplift people like us, we are missing Jesus.

We have the power within us through Christ to be an unstoppable force, especially when we rise and take action together. It's my hope that as we link arms and participate in grace together, we can charge our batteries up and bathe our families and communities in the light, love, and strength of our all-powerful and caring God.

Questions to Consider for Journaling and Discussion

1. How closely does your faith community resemble a global and diverse sisterhood?

2. How are you engaging in and amplifying the messages of our global sisterhood?

3. Who are you following and listening to that has a different story and background than your own?

4. How do you show up to conversations and situations that make you feel defensive with humility and openness?

8

Finding Energy

Dear Sister,

If there's one universal experience across womankind, it's utter exhaustion. For many of us, energy is a resource we covet as much as we do time and money. As we start to prioritize our own needs, we can begin to observe the natural flow of our energy. We can bring more intention to where we share it. We can acknowledge what people and activities build us up and give us energy and what people and activities drain us most. We can prioritize rest, and remember our worth does not lie in always doing.

I hope my experiences help you bring awareness to the seasons of your life and relationships and help you draw kind and loving boundaries when necessary.

Sending rejuvenation your way,
Megan

It seems that women have a special definition of the words "tired" and "exhausted." There is the exhaustion of a day of demanding labor, yes, or a day without a moment of respite, but I'm specifically referencing the complete emotional and physical exhaustion of pouring yourself into other people until you have nothing left. This might take days, weeks, months, or years, but it seems like so many of us get there; yet, the same people are still looking for more from us. We have, after all, taught them that we will always be there pouring ourselves out. I used to think this was holy. I thought this was sacrifice and surrender, those "S" words that have made my hair stand on end from well-meaning but misdirected sermons. It's heartbreaking to feel your God, whom you love more than life itself, is asking you to constantly be broken, exhausted, and depressed. It's even more demoralizing to feel your brothers and sisters in faith expect the same.

Thankfully, the more I get to know God, the less I see this at all supported by theology or what I know of God's nature. A God whose nature is love does not relegate God's followers and children to brokenness and exhaustion. We come to faith, to Christ, for meaning, for wholeness and community. What kind of faith do we have if we must constantly be burnt out to live it?

We do ourselves a disservice when we don't pay attention to the difference in physical and emotional energy. We can be physically exhausted, sure. Physical exhaustion is remedied by a night or sometimes, for the chronically exhausted, many nights of sleep. Emotional exhaustion and depletion can be far more challenging to combat and recover from. This is why I can spend a weekend doing absolutely nothing and still not feel ready or energized for my work week. Managing my emotional energy expenditure is a constant challenge.

My friend Erika is writing a book, pursuing grad school, and working full-time. She is crystal clear on where she is supposed to be. She shares about how she's navigating seasons in her life:

I have learned to say no without explaining myself, which is very hard. For all the ladies who are struggling with that, we feel you. You have to flex that muscle. One thing I have tried to do is write out plans. I draw my circle of what I know I'm called to in this season. In this season, I know God is calling me to write. God is calling me to study because I believe when the Holy Spirit teaches you, you can't teach something you don't know, and that requires isolation. For example, our church has this early-morning singing service. You come in and learn new songs once a month, and I don't attend. People could say I'm not a good Christian, but I need to nurture what is mine. That may be my writing time, my devotional time. I can't grow my talent if I don't invest it in my own soil. Too many times, we take the thing God has given us and just go, "Oh, look, there's a potluck; let me go" or "Oh, this person is doing something. I'm going," and you have not really done what God has asked you to do. So my boundary right now is saying no, and my other boundary is being home. I've learned that by being elsewhere, I'm not doing certain things.

You go through this season where your faith is attached to a lot of people and a lot of things, and I struggled for a bit when that season was dying because my faith was attached to people who I love and trust. My dad was my elder, my dad is my deacon, my dad is my preacher, so to contend with that was different than maybe for some people who more casually attend church. My faith was literally attached to very rooted, grounded people and also people I saw all the time. I would say the transition from adolescence into adulthood was really interesting for me, and just recently, I came fully out of it and can say I'm in a season of independence. My dad is still my preacher, but I own my faith. I've drawn the line, and everyone knows where I stand on every issue.

I think it was the hardest because I saw myself through the lens of other people for a long time. I don't think we're always honest as women about wearing multiple frames. You may take one off and think you see clearly and then realize you need to take something else off. This is really the first time I look in the mirror and I see my whole self, and I see myself for myself, and I'm doing it by myself. That means a lot to me. It made room for new relationships. God has brought so many wonderful people and women into my life who see different parts of me who other people couldn't see clearly or accurately. I can't even express the joy and gratitude I have for that. When I first thought about women's ministry, nobody was talking about it. So for God to bring women into my life that I can share my passions and ideas with has just been transformative. You have to cut ties to hold onto new things.

Here are some observations regarding emotional energy and how I have redirected mine to align more authentically with who I am and where I'm supposed to be.

For the Empaths...

I have felt the feelings of others from the time I was a little kid. I used to tell my family I did or didn't like a person's "atmosphere." I had strong feelings about the people I did and didn't like. Let's be real—I still do. I also remember time periods in family life by the general prevalent emotion. I always wanted to make my people feel better when they were sad or angry or frustrated. This was equally because I wanted to help and because I wanted to stop feeling their uncomfortable feelings. The only way I knew to be okay was to keep everyone around me okay as well.

This is exhausting and impossible. There are a lot of schools of thought on developing boundaries and grounding rituals around this. The mantra that has developed for me is "Their emotions are their responsibility, not mine." This doesn't mean I don't empathize or sit with people in difficult situations. This means I don't adopt their feelings as my own and carry them around all day or feel icky and depleted because of the interaction. This is hard. Some people call catching others' feelings empathy, but, really, it feels like an energy siphon that leaves you both depleted. For a long time, I thought I could ease others' pain by lying awake worrying about them at night or vividly feeling what they were feeling. The truth is only they can live out their story. I can't carry that for them. Empathy is holding space for them to carry and live their story how they are meant to. Empathy is sitting with them, listening. Sharing our presence with others in these moments is a valuable gift, and it is enough. It's not our job or place to fix things, to make everything okay. It is our job to show up when we can, authentically.

This was part of placing my worthiness in how helpful or needed I was. The more depleted I was emotionally the more worthy I felt because I was helping *so much*, when, in reality, I had misplaced worthiness and no understanding of how to manage my emotional energy. I also had no concept of how to receive healing or support because I found my worth in being a helper and giver.

Emotional Boundaries

The only way I have found to manage my emotional energy aside from carefully evaluating where I'm placing my worthiness is slowly and mindfully building internal boundaries. These are the most challenging boundaries. Often, we want the results that come with internal boundaries but have not built a framework in which we can implement them. So much of my identity was tied up in other people, what they thought of me, how they felt about themselves, their lives, if I could help at all, and managing those things for every person I met was overwhelming. Was it any wonder my circle was non-existent? There was no way I had the energy to keep that up with very many people at all. In contrast, building relationships out of authenticity is enriching not draining.

Writer and coach Neghar Fonooni once ran a program called The Bikini Rebellion. It was a week-long challenge with daily emails, journaling prompts, and a cue for Instagram posts to share themed around releasing the narrative that we need a specific kind of body to be worthy. Participating was transformative. I had already done a lot of body acceptance and self-image work, but her questions about where we are spending our energy were very telling for me. Neghar challenged us to look at our lives and see if we are spending our energy on things that authentically line up with who we are and our life's purpose. At that point, I was working a job with a lot of people I loved, but that was emotionally depleting on many levels. It was hard for me to acknowledge I was spending so much of my energy there and spending my weekends attempting to recover, only to do it all over again. I still don't put a big emphasis on life purpose because that can indicate we have one magic reason we are here, and if we miss it, we're screwed. Maybe we can and do have many life purposes. Multifaceted life purpose seems more nuanced and realistic. In any case, my job wasn't bringing me closer to mine anymore. There's this American ideal that "freedom" means doing whatever you want, and if you love something, you should magically be able to make money doing it. It could easily sound like I'm building up to "I quit my job, and now my life is free and amazing and creative!" I'm not. I like my house and needed to keep paying my mortgage, so instead of quitting my job, I started implementing targeted self-care and building more emotional boundaries.

I learned that as much as I hated mornings, what I did before I went into that workspace could make or break my resilience that day. I got really consistent with my morning rituals. It felt like having a buffer to others' stress and pain, allowing me to empathize without adopting it as my own. I started taking walks on lunch, getting out of the office to recharge, and I got really clear with myself on what my responsibilities actually were and where I was overextending myself emotionally. I did a lot of internal work, accepting that I am responsible for spending my energy, and others cannot take it unless I give it away. This is an empowering concept, but being in a helping field can sometimes feel like you're in a zombie movie. Instead of brains, the zombies suck out your life force. I'm not a parent, but I'm guessing parenting can feel like this, too. In reality, I can only offer up whatever my best is for that specific day. That has to be enough. Internalizing this gave me permission to set limits that I needed to and give myself a break. I did eventually shift to a position in a less emotionally charged specialty, which has been a great change, but I still value the boundaries I learned, and I implement them regularly.

There's a prevalent ideology going around that hustling hard and grinding is the only (and best) way to achieve our goals. I'll be the first to say that any goal worth having is not going to be quick or easy and will require certain amounts of commitment, but I think we often spend much of our energy hustling for goals that may not align with where we really need to be. There are a few reasons for this.

Misaligned Energy

The first is expecting permanence. "I'm doing this because it's what I've always done, and it's part of my identity." No external hobby or profession is required to be a permanent part of our lives if it isn't serving its purpose anymore. I have put so much energy into keeping projects and hobbies going when their season has long been over. We are not required to be some static, unchanging version of ourselves. If anything, growing through our seasons is a sign of maturity and wisdom. Like the sage gardener, we can watch over and celebrate every new sprout and honor those things that are finished blooming by clearing them away and making room for the next season's bounty. When we are in tune with our growth cycles, we can release control and recognize when a season is ending and when it's time to make room for something new. Those who use "You've changed" in an accusatory manner do not understand growth or are often afraid of it. I have regained so much energy and freedom by paying close attention to these seasons. If something isn't carrying the same joy or meaning anymore, I re-evaluate it.

This sounds simple but can be agonizing in practice. We acknowledge the seasons based on how much they impact our lives—how quickly the lawn grows or how much snow we have to shovel and whether we wear a sweater or parka, but the intelligent design of the seasons has so much more to offer than this. Themed through our very world and through all our myths and lore is this concept of the life/death/life cycle. We have this compulsion to grasp for a constant, for control, when, in reality, everything is in a constant cycle of growth, release, and renewal. We cause ourselves so much pain by clinging to what is ready for release. We ache for renewal but don't see that we must let go of what's over to make room for it. We pray for renewal in our lives and communities but resist the shake up, the release, the death. Admitting that life is in constant flux, change, and renewal is a hard lesson for this perfectionist and control freak, but once it starts seeping in, there is permission to relax, to release. Growth seasons can be hard but also often exciting as we feverishly chase down new opportunities and horizons. Renewal seasons are beautiful and expansive, but space must be curated for the season of release. Some things in our lives we may be glad to see go and leave behind. I have been happy to wave goodbye to seasons of job searching, working in retail (both for Chris and myself), working multiple jobs, seasons of depression, and basically every winter (usually coinciding with my depression. Hello seasonal affective disorder!). But other seasons have been harder for me to release because I identified so much of myself with them. I clung to powerlifting after my first meet was over, even though I was fully burnt out from it and needed a change. I have kept those clothes in the back of my closet that I knew would never fit my lifestyle or needs (or me) again, holding onto them "just in case." Here's the thing about letting go—When we surrender to it, it can actually be rejuvenating. Why is cleaning and purging unneeded belongings taking up extra space and energy so cathartic? It's a form of completing that cycle and making physical space for ourselves and for something new and needed.

I spent so much of my life being afraid of temporary. I structured myself around what I thought would last and who would stay. While commitment and longevity of relationship is important, I often couldn't fully enjoy or be present to what I had in my life because I was so worried about keeping it. Failing to acknowledge the play of seasons and life cycles throws us into a scarcity mindset, always scrambling to stay ahead of loss and lack in our lives.

The second reason is we often expect and crave linear timelines. Nancy Levin says, "Honor the space between no longer and not yet." This is where our lives happen, where growth happens, this sacred space between no longer and not yet. We cling so tightly to the goal, the idea of being finished somehow, when there's always another level and always farther to climb. It's okay if we aren't on a linear timeline. It's okay if our journey has deviances, dips, and valleys. That's where the messy magic happens. We need to put in work, yes, but if we spend all our time hustling and running around trying to get there faster, we miss the magic right in front of us, and we often miss our people.

The third is we are afraid of what will happen when we are still and quiet. We aren't ready to face where we really are and sit with our pain or loss. The busyness is white noise covering changes we know we need to make, vulnerabilities we need to step into or risks we need to take that terrify us. The hustling keeps us from thinking too hard or too deeply, from feeling too much. It's an off switch, a way to numb up and carry on with our lives without addressing our shadows and demons. In reality, that silent wild is where we can find the strength to reclaim what we need to reclaim and release what we need to release. The silent wild is where we must go to find the parts of ourselves we discarded when we thought being less would somehow make us enough.

Hustling for the sake of hustling and grinding is exhausting. For years, exercise and fitness were ways I worked through so many of these issues. I found that certain forms of working out made me feel powerful and validated. I liked seeing muscles popping out, being able to do and lift things people didn't expect someone my size to be able to lift and expanding, what "female" meant for myself. Through training regularly in Krav Maga and Brazilian Jiu Jitsu, I confronted my fear of being trapped, pinned down, unable to fight for myself. I learned that even when there's a 200-pound person holding me down, I don't stop fighting, and there's usually a way out. It made me tougher and more resilient, and I love it. However, I haven't worked out or gone to MMA classes in over a year because it was time for my energy to expand in new directions. I realized when that part of my life was draining more energy than it was giving. I am on hiatus. I'm sure I will be back at it eventually, but right now, the quiet and the stillness feel restorative. Seeing more of my husband and having time to spend on creative projects feels like what I need to be doing right now. I have long-term goals, which involve MMA heavily, but I am honoring that space between no longer and not yet.

When we are secure in our worthiness, comfortable asking for what we need, and comfortable saying yes and no when we mean it, we free up so much of our time and energy. We start aligning our activities and schedules authentically with who we were created to be. We can start tapping into creativity we didn't even know we had and finding deeper meaning in our relationships and our work. Something that has been incredibly healing for me is the creative work of other women.

Women Healing Women

Socially, it's our role and narrative to always be the physical and emotional caretakers not only of our children, but often of our men. Our performance is expected and not compensated. It's the price we pay for our worth in the order of patriarchy. This is overwhelming and exhausting, leading us to burn out and resent those in our lives we love.

This is why I find so much restoration in supporting, financially and personally, other women in their emotional labor and creative work. In balance, women taking care of each other and creating space for each other within their boundaries is beautiful and powerful. It's not only support of their lives and work, but an acknowledgement that emotional work is work. Emotional work is worth showing up and paying for. This looks like buying music, books, participating in events, showing up for our women and taking part in creating a healing community.

We prove our priorities by our purchases and our presence. I used to feel resentful having to spend money on creative experiences I wanted. Now, I place a high value on my personal growth and supporting and giving back to those who meet my needs in any way I can. Prioritizing these connections is another way to support the sisterhood. We need to be okay making some sacrifices and getting out of our comfort zones. This can look like clearing that weekend day or evening to be present with our sisterhood or driving somewhere out of the way for an event with people we don't know well yet. Giving up our resources of comfort and time counts, too. It's noticed, and it's valued. Don't expect the sisterhood to always fit your schedule. Make deliberate time and space in your schedule for sisterhood. This isn't a luxury that we can have if and when it's convenient. It's not a spa day; it's spiritual and emotional hygiene.

Erika describes the intention in her relationships with mentors and encouragers:

> *There are two women who I really love, and I think they truly were sent by God at the right time to encourage me. Both of them are older than me. Both my grandmothers have passed away, and I've always missed that thing that people have when they can go home for holidays and see their grandmother because there's wisdom in age, and I've always wished I would have had a grandparent to talk to me in different seasons of my life. So there's one woman I'm thinking of. She mails me encouragement, CDs postcards, prays for me, speaks life into me. Sometimes we are so quick to speak*

a negative word or tell someone what they're thinking is unreasonable, but she always tells me that I can do it. There's another sister in Christ who is older than me as well, and she's always super excited about everything I do. Because she prays for me, when she says things, I know it's affirmation from God. So I might be thinking about something, and she'll come to me and be like, "Hey, I just had this idea of you on a stage speaking to women," and I'll be like, "Girl, I was just making notes for a 500-person event." That's how you know there's a spiritual realm working on your behalf. So those two women I know pray for me, and it's not flippant; I know they're doing it.

I have been very intentional about developing strong female relationships, and I'd say they are microspaces. I don't really hang out with fifteen women unless it's an event, but I am very intentional about one-on-one time with women. Whether it's texting facetiming, it's very important, regardless of what's going on, to have good girlfriends. I grew up without a sister, so I fumbled through a lot of those relationships. I look back and wonder why I said and did things. But now, I can look at my life and say I can be myself, my broken self, in those microspaces. There's one girl I can text and just say, "I'm feeling a mess," and she'll say, "Me, too." Those microspaces get me through the day to build the content. You may not need a lot of people. You may need one person to walk around the beach with, to debrief with.

I work to be intentional about my purchases. Most of my workout and lounge wear come from a size-inclusive brand started to empower women and combat negative advertising and photoshop used to target our self-esteem. I haven't bought anything from Victoria's Secret in years, favoring small, female-owned lingerie companies that create beautiful items for a large size range and have advertising practices I can support. My favorite affirmation cards are created by Erin Brown, and I *do* appreciate her guidance and wisdom in my walk and life. I use every chance I get to gift those cards as well as her books, which I love. Certain albums from female artists play on repeat for me, all different, vibrant expressions of nuance, challenge, and triumph. I have purchased mindset courses, books, and CDs, and I have attended Christian women's retreats. I don't share any of this to raise myself up as any kind of standard. I share it because I think, so often, we wonder where to start and what supporting each other really looks like. Supporting women financially may look different for you. I know in my gut when something is important for me to contribute to and participate in. Every time I have done this, I have been glad I did and blown away by the content offered. So many women are delving into their lives and experiences to present astonishing work.

It's also important to make sure we are not only supporting women whose stories and pictures are similar to our own. If we are going to keep building this radiant community, remember, we all need to be there.

Daydream with me for a minute. What would faith and sisterhood feel like if:

- We all only said yes and no when we were 100 percent behind it?
- We had the energy to show up for ourselves and each other?
- We saw other women not as our competition or judges, but as powerful sisters in arms who have each other's backs?
- Shame was never promoted as faith?
- We loved on each other's families and communities?

- We could show the world what true love and community look like in action?
- Our words and actions carried weight because they were always authentic?
- We were focused on taking up more space and expanding our community?
- We never worried about shrinking our messes or our waistlines?
- Our kids saw us living big, bold, vulnerable, and love-filled lives?
- We knew our gut instincts were instilled in us by an all-knowing Creator and revered them?
- We celebrated all aspects of femininity, the bloody, the dirty, the wild, the soft, the delicate, as not only aspects of ourselves but shared aspects of our Creator?

This isn't just a dream. It's already happening. The question is do we want it to happen in *our* community? Are we ready to get vulnerable, commit to show up, and discover who we were made to be?

Questions to Consider for Journaling and Discussion

1. How do you manage your emotional energy on a day-to-day basis?

2. Are you spending your emotional energy taking on others' feelings that are theirs to manage?

3. Who are you supporting with your presence and purchases?

4. How are you making space and time in your life for sisterhood?

5. How are you compensating other women's emotional labor and energy?

6. How have you seen seasons shift and change in your life?

7. How have you handled releasing old seasons to make way for renewal?

9

Claiming Renewal: Building New Tables

Dear Sister,

Do you know how powerful women are who know themselves and know the vision they cast in their communities? We are the culture makers and world changers. We've talked about deconstructing oppressive belief systems, prioritizing community, creating safe and brave spaces, and using our social powers for good.

I'm excited because in this chapter we talk about pulling it all together and building this whole and healed world. Like everything worthwhile in life, it's going to take time and effort, but I've found there's nothing I'd rather be spending my time and effort doing.

Writing this book has changed my life. It has pushed me to live its message in new ways. I've had so many opportunities to experience the power and wonder of women bringing their gifts together because this book taught me to look for them. I hope it does the same for you. I hope you gain deep support and nourishment through spaces of sisterhood. I hope you develop and share your gifts because they are so needed.

Looking forward to writing the next chapter with you,
Megan

I remember sitting in my therapist's office, asking her if she thought my goals for a grounded and mindful life were realistic. I didn't want to bother attempting this journey, getting my hopes up, if this didn't actually happen for people. If there was a chance, though, I was willing to put in the work. I have spent years working reclamation into my daily life. The constant evaluation and questioning are almost second nature to me now. Renwal is a newer, welcome season greeting me with fresh creativity and opportunities for community and relationship. Renewal is part of our spiritual life cycle. So often, we are experiencing renewal in one aspect of life while still actively seeking reclamation in another. As with all things, it's layered and nuanced.

In the beginning, my goal for personal growth was just to be in a place where I felt secure, not plagued by constant anxiety and depression. I wanted to be free to express my autonomous, authentic self. This is a great first goal, but it is just the first, the start. There is so much more to life, and especially life in faith, than just finding "okay." I spent several years enacting boundaries in my life, clumsily at first. I ruffled some feathers figuring out how to flex my new autonomy muscles. As I learned how to find groundedness, my Divine Parent gently started challenging me to step out of my comfort zone.

Boundaries Vs. Comfort Zones

We tend to say boundaries and mean comfort zone, and they are not the same. Boundaries are what is and isn't okay with us and how we communicate that. We can and should grow in our boundaries, and they may change depending on our season. Our comfort zones only get smaller unless we continually, gently stretch them. Renewal is the fruit of stepping out of our comfort zones when we are led in full autonomy and participating in community. Renewal is the outworking of abundant blessings and fulfillment of promises. Renewal is finding and celebrating the fruits of the spirit in our own lives.

Reclamation and renewal are sisters. Reclamation is our intention, our pursuit, and our commitment. Renewal grows from this. Renewal springs up from a reclaimed identity with fresh creativity and vibrance. Reclamation is the messy part, the retraining of our lives and thought patterns, the constant sifting of what we claim and what no longer serves us. Renewal is the juicy, sweet fruit that grows out of those efforts.

It took me several years of practicing reclamation to even dream of there being more than okay. I have always been overwhelmed with the idea of finding life purpose, or calling, or personal mission. There are so many books and articles on finding your sweet spot and living a fulfilling life. What I am finding is that my calling and mission were what started growing once I cultivated my life through reclamation.

Erin Brown once said in regard to feminism, "We don't need a seat at the table; we're building new tables." This stuck with me, the difference in mindset between fighting for something that should already be ours but is held by someone else and just going out and building something new, creative, and amazing out of what we've been collectively handed. This is the difference between reacting to injustice and being proactive about building the world we need.

Often, Christian women don't identify with leadership because we so rarely see it modeled. We are taught to look to the men and follow, so this building new tables is unknown territory. We are so often uncomfortable even leading a devotional or a prayer because women's leadership is rarely a focus of the church. We learn that our voices are not welcome, that we should be quiet and reserved in the worship of our God. Women's programs struggle for many reasons (several of them are covered in the "Finding Sisterhood" chapter), but I find this lack of female leadership and lack of female representation in leadership to be key as well.

There are many in-depth studies on the New Testament roles of women in church community and worship settings with varied conclusions and theological outcomes resulting in a sliding scale of women's involvement in the leadership in faith communities. I grew up in fairly conservative churches with all male preachers and teachers with the exception of women's events. I never really questioned this, felt the men were doing a bad job, or had a desire to be up front teaching and sharing (partially because I didn't see women doing this and partially because I'm an introvert). I'm realizing, now, how much this affected not only my faith but my development across the board in terms of taking leadership and initiative. Taking a step back and looking at the fruit of masculine-only leadership is often sobering.

Maybe I'm missing something, but from my pew, I often see women feeling overwhelmed, underappreciated, and unseen. Continuation of archaic patriarchal structures not modeled in descriptions of New Testament leadership or relationships lead women into staying in abusive relationships because of incorrect teachings on submission and autonomy. I see women not developing their gifts fully (or at all sometimes); men shouldering more than needed and getting burnt out; men and women missing out on vibrant female led ministries; devaluing women, their ministries, and teaching women their autonomy and voice do not matter.

I have never found evangelical Christianity's teachings on women to bring freedom. Being a Christian woman is wonderful. It's also intensely painful and lonely at times. It's a scary thing to be led and gifted in encouragement and building communities and always be wondering where and when the no will fall. I have been incredibly blessed to speak and share within my local church community, but I still wonder ... What will be the limit of my service? Where will my worship be constrained? How and when will I be silenced? This is the legacy Christian femininity gifts me. These aren't "if" questions. They aren't saying, "Oh, this might happen." My experience and that of other women has taught me these are questions of when. The beliefs of men in church leadership hold the power to unleash my gifts as a woman in that community or suppress them. They stand between me and service, and, in many ways, it feels like between God and me. Sadly, many Christian women I know end up so debilitated by not understanding their true worth in faith that their gifts remain completely buried. Many have even left faith behind. They couldn't find the expanse of their Creator in the confines and limits of their church, so they set it all aside.

I wish that instead of telling us what our role is based on a handful of cherry-picked bible verses, church leadership would ask *us* about our callings. Perhaps this is a better way to determine what women's roles should be. Instead of showing us a box in which our service and worship must be contained, trust our relationships with God, and trust God in our lives to bring about the service and ministry God has for us. If, indeed, it is scriptural for us to always stay in the shadow of men, there should be no concern that God will lead us to anything else. But if we have developed these beliefs based on interpretations steeped in patriarchal culture, there may be a whole expanse of creative ministry and service awaiting us we have yet to explore and claim.

What if limiting women is actually a warfare strategy of our enemy designed to incapacitate, minimize, and shut down over half the church? When I read *Divided by Faith* by Michael O. Emerson and Christian Smith, I was devastated to learn a broader history of the church and abolition. My faith traditions were, at one point, used to erase the culture and spirituality of an entire group of people and ensure their subjugation through verses like "Slaves, obey your masters" (Eph 6:5-9, NKJV).

Many Old Testament laws were also especially concerning in regard to slavery. It was a fight for hundreds of years, but now, we have different understanding and perspectives on those texts. The fruit of dehumanization and slavery has never been the fruit of the Spirit. We know it's wrong; we feel it in our bones. There are far more references to the roles of slaves in the Bible than there are the roles of women, but now, this is our hold out.

I appreciate the translation of The Message in general but especially in discussion of the fruits of the Spirit:

> *But what happens when we live God's way? He brings gifts into our lives, much the same way that fruit appears in an orchard—things like affection for others, exuberance about life, serenity. We develop a willingness to stick with things, a sense of compassion in the heart, and a conviction that a basic holiness permeates things and people. We find ourselves involved in loyal commitments, not needing to force our way in life, able to marshal and direct our energies wisely. Legalism is helpless in bringing this about; it only gets in the way. (Galatians 5:22-24)*

Does that sound like a picture of Christian femininity? Affection for others, exuberance about life and serenity? At times, I have found more fruit of the Spirit from secular authors and more sacred feminine connection and community than I have found in the church. I don't think this means they have something we don't, but I think it means we can easily miss aspects of God and faith that are staring us in the face. I realized as I started writing this book that it is easy for me to get more soul food from secular women than Christian women. Sometimes they feel safer when healing from Christian patriarchy. Sometimes they seem more accessible.

My friend Kelly summarizes how participating in church as a woman of faith felt:

> *It feels extremely superficial. Really pretty on the exterior, in a neat and pretty box, but a mess on the inside. As long as everything looked put together, it was okay and acceptable. There's a lot of shame in the church associated with women. If you aren't behaving a certain way or if your household or marriage isn't a certain way, you aren't accepted in certain circles. It's not inclusive. I felt that I spent most of my time, instead of being free, trying to fit in and trying to make myself acceptable to this group of women who I so desperately needed to belong to, to be accepted in the church. It was very stressful. I'm not saying people were mean or anything, but it was a shame-based structure and dynamic. People aren't even aware they're doing it. You're just expected to behave, and look, and act a certain way. Oftentimes, it was completely different at home.*

I am learning that we find what we look for. Realizing I wanted more of a faith focus in my personal growth, I began praying female leadership into my life. In the span of a week, I discovered multiple amazing Christian women who have global ministries, businesses, and nonprofits. Of course, there's nothing wrong with consuming creative work of non-Christian women, and many of them are preaching a gospel of love they don't name, but I'm learning that for true grounding in faith, we also need to walk with our women of faith. Christian women's ministries can sometimes hold narrow offerings, but if we refuse to engage them, none of us will grow. Those in leadership won't know our needs if we don't speak up, and we shut down our own potential growth by not engaging them and sharing our needs. Sometimes noticing a glaring need or deficiency can be our call to ministry.

I have been ruminating on why it's sometimes easier to stay disconnected or to reach out on more surface levels with those you don't share spirituality with, and I think it comes down to vulnerability. So often, the closer I am with someone, the harder a time I have had sharing intimate details with them. The closer I am with them, the harder it will be for me if they decide they don't like something I say, if they choose to leave. When I was a teenager not sharing with my family, I just thought they didn't understand or get me. On some levels, there was a lot they didn't understand about me but often because I chose not to share with them. At that time, I was pouring myself out to a more anonymous friend online who I could shut inside the laptop if we had a disagreement, not that we ever really did past whether romance was dead. (I was the staunchly practical, he, the defender of romance.) When that friend became my husband years later (yes, yes, romance won after all), I found myself more hesitant to share what was really going on, even though he has never been anything but supportive and affirming. This was a call to vulnerability for me. During my most challenging struggle with depression (the one I finally went to therapy for), I hadn't shared any of it until I decided I needed therapy. I hid my struggle for months from the closest person to me because I was worried about how it would affect him. He would later joke and ask about my day, and when I said, "good" or "okay," he would follow up with, "Does that mean secretly terrible?"

I think we deal with something similar in the church sometimes. We avoid sharing because we are most worried about the ramifications of our vulnerability with the communities that impact our lives the most. The risk involved personally if I read a secular author and disagree is minimal. The risk involved if a Christian says things about God or my relationship with God that feels wrong or violating is much greater, much harder for me to deal with. What we so often forget about in this conversation, though, is the payoff of vulnerability when it's done right, the magic created when we actually hold safe spaces to share.

Over the last few years, I have been working on both building the boundaries necessary to share myself safely and taking steps to share with those who have earned the right to hear my story. It's hard. Sharing like this in carefully constructed and thought out concepts is easier for me. Sharing with people I don't know or may never meet is easier for me. The hard part about this process will be sharing with the people I am close to. Those whose eyes I will look into after they read it and know all my vulnerable spaces. Will they use it against me? Will they reject me because we may have theological differences? Will I see veiled judgement in their eyes, or will it bring us closer? Will it feed and give more life to a growing community of vibrant and loving women doing life together? Only taking this risk will tell.

I have often felt that I didn't have anything of note to create, to add to this work of rebuilding and expanding the sacred feminine for us all, but here I am. I'm still not sure this is of note or really anything that will be read by anyone but myself and my mom, but I needed to create it. It needs to be said. I have watched Christian women my entire life. We are some of the hardest working, most devoted women I have ever known but so often shut down. I have seen the dark side of fundamentalism and legalism, the abuse and carnage that runs rampant when we start idolizing people and systems over God. Unfortunately, women often suffer the fallout most severely. I stopped being surprised when my girlfriends confided to me that they had histories of abuse. If I can offer any light, comfort, friendship, or space to any woman on a journey home to herself, I want to.

I want to see more women—actually, no, *all* women—building new tables. I get goosebumps thinking about the love and community we can create and spread together. The tastes of it that I have already had are healing and rejuvenating. I need more in my life, but most, I want to see all my women living out the full and expansive versions of themselves they were created to be. I want your art, your community, your creations, projects, and vision. I need your voice, energy, and intuition in my life.

Remember what's inside you, germinating in the soft, dark places. The book you have been writing for years in your head, the community center you see when you drive by that empty building, the songs you sing by yourself in your car or when you're cooking. Pay attention. Always take your next step, but always honor the journey and that space of "not yet." Share your journey with your sisters; we get there faster together. Jo Saxton says in her book *The Dream of You,* "When the grit and the guts of your broken identity meet the grace and goodness of God, it will reveal you, but He will transform you. You're in Him now, with all His resources available to you. You have access to His power, mercy, and grace."[14] The magic is God re-membering us piece by piece.

It's easy to let imposter syndrome take over, the sneaking thoughts of "What if I'm wrong?" "What if I can't?" "What if nobody cares?" or worse, "What if I'm attacked for this?" These thoughts have never been of God in my life. The times I have been wrong, couldn't, or shouldn't, it was clear, obvious, and without shame. So many times, though, I have not reached out or made connections because I was intimidated, jealous, or made assumptions about the people I was drawn to. Assumptions like "They're too busy" or "They won't be interested in anything I have to share." Attempting to take control or head off responses of others is dangerous and limiting. After listening to Jen Hatmaker's book *Of Mess and Moxie,* I moved on to her *For the Love* podcast. One of the first episodes in her "For the Love of Girlfriends" series featured Shasta Nelson, who has built a company around helping people find deep connection and friendship. Shasta quantifies how deep our relationships are through the factors of how safe and seen we feel and how satisfied we are with the relationship overall. She quantifies how we participate in them through the categories of initiation, consistency, positivity, and vulnerability. This was the first time I had really stopped to think about what kind of friend I really am.

My trust issues from childhood defaulted me as a responder not an initiator. This left me constantly trying to manage relationships that I wasn't actually putting active energy into, and as a result, they weren't very fulfilling. I remember one of the first times I initiated an organic hangout. I reminded myself all the way to my friend's house, *She could have said no; it's up to her to be honest about what she wants.* The more I have initiated, the more comfortable I have gotten with it, and the quieter the anxious and negative voices have become. I didn't realize that my own insecurities were locking down my ability to connect authentically. I really love Shasta's work because she breaks down relationships into concrete, manageable terms. Now I have a much better understanding on when I'm being called to and/or really *want* to reach out and follow that nudge. I don't attach to an answer or outcome. I am fulfilling my goal of living authentically just by opening the door.

Our friendships also tell the story of our histories, the women who encouraged us, moms who modeled sisterhood for us, the women we were mentored by and mentored from young ages.

In our interview, I asked Jamie about her role models and mentors. She shared:

> *I've been so lucky to have beautiful, strong, amazing women in my life. One woman, whom I only realized a couple years ago how big her impact was on my life, was Lisa Bolizzi. She was one of the first people who really saw me as a young person and connected with me as an older woman. She intentionally mentored me and spoke so much love into my life. I can point to her as one of*

the original people who showed me the Kingdom of God. We have a mutual friend named Michele Urban who I've shared the same kind of connection with. Martha Pawloski came to me at critical points in my life. She's a nurturer.

My own mother is such a strong woman and an amazing example. I've always had really powerful female friendships, but I watched a mom who had great connections with other women. She was always on the phone or meeting up. She didn't sacrifice her female friendships as we were growing up. The friendships I had as a kid were because their mom was friends with mine. We all became family to each other because the moms always wanted to hang out. She's still a very connected person and maintains friendships. She showed me how to be a connected woman, and I'm so grateful to have had a mom like that. She's a badass.

I have a great example in a mother-in-law, too. She is very nurturing but also has this inner stability that I don't come by naturally. I have to work for that centering because I'm kind of a spazz. But I watch her, and I get this sense of groundedness. And I'm so glad she passed that on to her son, who is my husband. I've just had this rockstar lineup of women in my life. It's been wonderful.

Right now, I'm thirty-five, and I like to think I'm not like, too old to be cool. I'm recognizing the power I have in connections with girls who are eighteen to twenty-two. I actually have some really strong connections with girls in that age group, and I love them, and I root for them. I find myself inviting them more and more into my life because we are benefitting from each other. I'm so grateful someone did that for me through that period of my life.

It's intergenerational. I invite these girls into my home who live in my neighborhood, but my daughter, who is ten, looks up to them because they're eighteen. I see the way my daughter looks at them, and they don't recognize what an impact their acceptance and love and affirmation has on her. They build her up in a way I'll never be able to because I'm just "Mom." I watch the way these young girls are speaking into her life, and I'm so grateful she has solid, amazing women. We also both know Mallorie Urban. I've had this beautiful connection with her. I used to babysit Mallorie when I was little, and her mom was a mentor to me, and now she babysits my kids. Now, she's in law school kicking butt and taking names. I talk to my daughter about possibilities for her life, and I say "Look, look at Mallorie. She's at Stanford Law School. The possibilities are endless for you, kid."

Wild female friendship doesn't sprout out of waiting for another woman to initiate contact. It doesn't come from "Oh, hey, we should get together some time." It comes from showing up in needed ways in each other's lives daily. It's care packages and text messages, ugly selfies, and Facetime chatting. It's book clubs, favorite music, watching and cheering on each other's growth. It's plant swaps, cooking together, and sharing a bottle of wine. Watching, praying, and crying over each other's families. It's co-parenting. This is the ground floor, down and dirty of female leadership. We lead by showing up, first for ourselves then for our communities. I used to think leadership took a special vision or gift. I've learned that the leaders I watch and respect so much are the ones consistently showing up for their people.

My friend Erika has a strong calling to unite and liberate women. When I asked her who she was paving the way for and what tables she is building, she shared:

> *I'm paving the way for any young woman who has a dream. I don't think we really sit down and think intentionally about what it's like to have dormant dreams. I have met so many older women who are just like, "I don't have anything." I'm like what a lie. The God of the universe, who doesn't even replicate the stripes on a zebra, has made all these women in the world, and you wanna tell me He made you with nothing? It doesn't make sense. I am paving the way for women to first investigate that. I'm all about finding your purpose, fasting for your purpose, writing down the things God does week to week. I'm paving the way for women to courageously pursue that. Unadulterated, yes, you will be trembling. Yes, you will be nauseous. Yes, you will lose sleep, but I am paving the way for women to do the thing.*

There are two separate but related definitions of the word "practice." There's the verb that I loathed as a child: "Practice: repeated exercise in or performance of an activity or skill so as to acquire or maintain proficiency in it." And the noun: "Practice: as in having a practice to actively pursue or be engaged in (a particular profession or occupation)." [15]

I think we need to embrace both kinds of practice to build wholehearted, vibrant communities. Words that become tiresome like "practice" and "maintenance" can be so beautiful and deep. The work of honing a skill is a time honored tradition, and as we come into ourselves, the women we were created to be, we continually practice our boundaries, our autonomy, and, brick by brick, building our communities—building new tables. Maintenance is something we talk about with sighs when discussing property or cars, but really, think about it. We *get* to spend energy taking care of what we love. We *get* to put energy into maintaining relationships with those we care about. If maintenance becomes a drag, either we are maintaining things that no longer serve our greater purpose, or we need to reconnect with why they are really important.

We can say we see the need for stronger communities of Amazonian sisters in arms, but these communities are built of the daily. They are built of showing up for each other, of not being afraid to initiate connection, to take that risk. They are built of spontaneous pizza parties and book clubs and doing life together. They are built of late night texts when life is too hard and too real, finding the solace to get up the next morning and start just one more time, and the time after that, and the time after that.

Building community is one of those concepts that sounds fantastic and inspiring, and then when it's time to roll up our sleeves, we often aren't sure just where to start or what to do. We may have inspiration and vision but lack the team or support necessary to sustain it through the long haul. This can feel discouraging and even more isolating. Everyday life and demands crowd out our initial excitement and fervor as we realize our schedules are already over committed and exhausting. I am learning that in the beginning, baby steps of communal growth, showing up for each other is the foundation. If there's something fundamental to practice, it's just showing up when we are led. I have set an intention to reach out when I'm thinking of someone, send a text, email or card just to let them know they are on my heart. Sometimes it seems we overcomplicate things. Every parent knows the most powerful way of investing in their child's life is consistently showing up, being there when they have a need, get home from school, have games, shows, and graduations. Putting energy into showing up is the first step. The best way we can build rapport in our communities is by finding ways to show up for people individually in needed ways. Much of our society is built on inaction. Convenience is a god we often turn to, centering our needs and wants over building bridges and connections. We want to build a space, a ministry so often without putting in the personal work of showing up for others first. When we show up for others, we remind ourselves that this work is about edifying and uplifting them, not about fulfilling our own aspirations.

When I first felt called to women's ministry, I thought first of what I could offer—devotionals, programs—and what spaces I could create. The questions I am pondering now feel like those I should have started with: How can I uplift, support, and celebrate the women in my community? What needs can I meet without requiring energy or additional time from them? My ministry is not the important thing here; building connection is. What are they passionate about that I can cheer on or enrich? This is the crux of leadership. We must keep reaching forward to those women who have been there already and reaching back to those coming up behind us. We must learn to be both student and teacher. Sitting at the feet and the tables of those women who are in the life stages ahead of ours but still being ready to share and encourage those just beginning to navigate what we have long been practicing. I am not discouraging starting ministries or creating new spaces for communal growth. If anything, that's the goal, but we often overlook this first step.

As we do life together, we naturally begin to fulfill the great commission. Our lives are gospel, love-filled lives. Our sisterhood and the love generated spills into our greater communities. They see warm, whole, loving, authentic relationships. They see acceptance. We share our faith through our creativity, our mutual hobbies and passions. We have the opportunity, together, to light a path home for them to be the person they were created to be.

Questions to Consider for Journaling and Discussion

1. What women are in your circle that you would like to deepen your relationships and friendships with?

2. How can you show up for them?

3. What do you feel is missing or lacking in your faith community?

4. How are you being called to speak and move into that space?

5. What obstacles stand in your way?

Dear Sister,

Thank you so much for the time and energy you've spent reading this book. I hope it challenged you. I hope it affirmed you. I would love to hear your feedback. Find me on Instagram: @mwooding or Facebook https://www.facebook.com/meganewooding/, or email me at meganewooding@gmail.com.

I want to hear about your communities of sisterhood, your calling, and your passions. I want to hear how you came home to yourself.

Can't wait to connect in the next chapter,

Megan

Recommended Reading

Be the Bridge - Latasha Morrison

If you read one of these books, read this one. *Be the Bridge* is personal expose, history lesson, and game plan for faith-based racial reconciliation. Latasha's presentation is accessible to all audiences, and she wrote this book for such a time as this.

The Dream of You - Jo Saxton

Biblical reconstruction of our identities in Christ with leading questions and concepts to grow roots and take hold of our worthiness more fully. Fantastic starting point if you're just starting to think about identity, autonomy, and worthiness. Really amazing refresher if you've been on this path a while. My favorite thing about this book is Jo's in-depth understanding of scripture and faith and the comprehensive unearthing of how massive a topic identity is to Christianity.

The Gifts of Imperfection - Brene Brown

This was my starting point. I championed my perfectionism until I read this book and realized it was draining my life force. Brene introduces some hard but vital topics through research-based study of shame and vulnerability. Contrasting her personal experiences and stories of those she knows with her research is a powerful combination. My biggest takeaway was the realization that the armor of coping mechanisms I had built to keep myself safe in my life were, in reality, suppressing my growth and isolating me. My quest for fully authentic living and relationship was born out of this book.

Braving the Wilderness - Brene Brown

If I had to use one word to describe this book, it would be "timely." I feel like this should be required reading for anyone who wants to share any thoughts on political discourse or who wants a Facebook account. This is not about politics specifically but about how we align ourselves with different groups because we need connection in our lives but end up trying to fit in instead of finding true belonging. We bunker up with our group and miss out on meaningful and needed nuance and growth because we fall into "us vs. them" mentalities, and the idea of standing up to our group when we disagree is terrifying because we have seen the dehumanization that those who dissent are subject to. I found this book *incredibly* grounding in a socially tumultuous time. Lots of nuggets in relation to finding true belonging and exercising authenticity in community.

Half the Church - Carolyn Custis James

I listened to this audiobook driving to visit my family. I kept yelling at the steering wheel in agreement with how spot on it is! Carolyn takes a global approach to women's ministry, highlighting the atrocities still oppressing literally millions of women (conservatively) through the global south. This was published in 2011 but is as timely as ever.

Just Show Up - Kara Tippetts & Jill Lynn Buteyn

My mom sent me this little gem a year or two ago. It's co-written by a woman with cancer and one of her best and most supporting friends and confidants. It's about showing up for people (shocker, I know) and all that entails when you're not sure how to help or if you even belong in that space. It's about finding and building an authentic faith community from open and vulnerable spaces. Showing up has become a theme in my life, and I think this little book had a hand in that.

Letters to Lola - Erin Brown

Erin wrote *Letters to Lola* as a collection of essays/letters to her daughter. It is everything I wish I knew about womanhood when I was a preteen. From dealing with depression to self-care and learning autonomy, reading this was like going back and lovingly coaching the parts of myself that still felt like a confused, isolated thirteen-year-old girl. I gave it to a young friend of mine and told her it's the parts of womanhood that often go unexplained and so often trip us up when we are still figuring out who we are in life. I think this is great for the adolescent girl in all of us and also for our adolescent girls.

Sovereign - Erin Brown

Sovereign is about reclamation. Half poetry, half essays, this little book is a powerhouse, a feminist manifesto. It has some strong language, so be aware if that bothers you. It is a rally cry, a call to sisters in arms, piercingly honest and refreshingly authentic. I found this book so motivating to keep claiming my autonomy and creating new platforms and spaces for an empowered feminine community.

I'm Still Here - Austin Channing Brown

Austin shares her experience of claiming her identity as a black woman in the church and the many barriers she had to overcome in ministry and her career. Austin's narrative is engaging, and her challenges are faced by many.

The Women Who Run with Wolves - Clarissa Pinkola Estes

This is a secular research-based book focusing on feminine myth and folk stories, the underlying themes they hold and the deeper meanings behind them. I have found it a fascinating study, peeling back layers of the feminine psyche and seeing the themes that weave themselves through cross culturally.

Jesus Feminist - Sarah Bessey

I was reaching a crisis of faith when I read/listened to this book. My faith journey was leading me deeper into the love and creativity of a wild and passionate God but leading me away from longheld preconceived ideas of a God prejudiced against women. I asked myself a lot of hard questions about whether I was just making myself a more acceptable version of God but then if God *were* patriarchal primarily it would cancel out so much of what is documented and written as God's nature. *Jesus Feminist* made me cry happy tears, listening to account after account of how Jesus treated His women throughout His ministry and after. This book delved into the scripture that confirmed what God had been revealing.

Of Mess and Moxie - Jen Hatmaker

This was a book club book and my introduction to Jen Hatmaker. If you get the chance to listen to Jen read the audiobook, do it. She is amazing and hilarious, and you'll feel like her newest girlfriend by the end. This book was incredibly affirming, and what struck me most was Jen's description of community and friendship in her life. She talks about how her people do life together, and it is inspiring. She also has a podcast called *For the Love*, which has introduced me to many other amazing women, Jo Saxton among them.

Divided by Faith - Michael O. Emerson & Christian Smith

This book taught me how much I didn't know about the intersection of church and racial history. It was a deep dive and incredibly educational. It's research based but not unapproachable. It details not only church history, but also the current challenges so many of our congregations face across denominations searching for racial reconciliation.

Learning to Walk in the Dark - Barbara Brown Taylor

Okay, *all* of BBT's books are impactful, and you should read them. However, this one was a particular balm to me as I battled seasonal depression. Barbara explores our antipathy to darkness and highlights why darkness is actually necessary for our flourishing.

Glorious Weakness – Alia Joy

My friend Jaime (who you now know pretty well) suggested this book. It's a moving exploration of real faith in all the messy places of life. In grief, in poverty, in faith community that lacks self-awareness and empathy. Alia shares her experiences from being a suicidal missionary kid with undiagnosed bipolar disorder, to caring for her aging parents and finding strength and comfort in faith through her times of weakness.

Acknowledgements

Dear Sister was made possible by sisterhood and community, which is one of my favorite things about it. Special thanks to Kelly Gustafson Sexton, Erika Kimberly Stanley, Jaime Fisher, Heather Heath, and Pamela Conklin (Mom) for sharing your stories and experiences through interviews. We are starting important conversations. I could not have written this book without the constant support of my friend Chilan. Thank you for listening to all my rants, affirming me, and sending me care packages and gift cards for mac and cheese. Thanks to Kimberly Cruz Lopez, and Kelly Cutchin for reminding me that this is necessary and important work every solitary time I doubted myself. A special thank you to my husband, Chris, who has become one of the most grounding influences in my life and work. Thank you for always reminding me that I am enough. Thank you to my editor and self-publishing expert, Monique D. Mensah with Make Your Mark Publishing Solutions for helping me make *Dear Sister* the best it can be. Thank you to my online community for your constant support and engaging with me. I'm so glad you're here.

Special thanks to those who backed the Kickstarter campaign to fund the editing and publishing of *Dear Sister*: Keith Smith, Chris Wooding, Mike & Pam Conklin, Michelle & John Wooding, Liza Hedegaard, Roberta O'Grady, Michelle Hanks, Denise

D'Aniello, Kelly Gustafson Sexton, Amy Hull, Ashley Wooding, Errol & Mickey DeLott, Rebecca Crowley, Kelly Vineyard, Jesse Conklin & Rachel Oshlag, Bambi Lynn, Cynthia, Chilan Ngo, Gina Benevento, The Heath Family, Michelle R. Barzallo, Danielle Schmitt, Lindsay O'Connor, Johan Fredrik Holst, Alexzandra Thomas, Mallorie Urban, Krystal Collard, Hannah Duarte, Helen & Marc, Serrae Reed, Christine, J. Auble, Kimani Sioux, Laura R, Rebecca Emery, Valerie Eyerly, Annie Singer, Amanda Lepley Simard, Coralys Santana, Nikki Nieves, Paula Freeman, Lee Lee, Sue Fournier, Shirley Chock, Abby Valletta, Amy Fountain, Linda Reeves, Marie Morris, Claudia Bayer, Liz Beaver, Kalyn Z, Rosa L. Hernandez, Sydney Stauffer, Marlaina Watton, Jeannette, Bridget Paddock, Brittanie Smith, Josie Banks, Jen Sinkler, Sonia Garcia, Monique D. Mensah, Bethany Samperi, Virginia, Sarah Storck, Rebecca Foley, Amelia Ikeda, Camille Boyd, Heather Posey Eddy, Lynn Butkus, Kelly Cutchin, Jennifer Greer, Heather Heath, Krista David, Angela Devlen, Becky Aldi, Jonathan Woodard, Jaime Fisher, Priscilla Thomas, Lauren Johnston, Kristin Hernandez, Chelsey, Julie Musgrove, Nicole Littletaylor, Ted Blaine, Cindy Navarro, Sara Skudzienski, Wilton Carraway Jr., Janice Yale, Martha Pawloski, Melissa Tarutis, Pam Carlie Holiday, Melissa Fenner, Tina Caplan, Ashley Anne Clark, Denise, Nancy Vidro, Marion & Volker, Patricia Kern, Nicole LaVette, Alyssa Levy, Samantha, Monica Simpson, Jolene Tolbert, and Cathie Dager. Thank you for believing this book needs to be in the world.

Notes

1. Brene Brown PHD, LMSW *Rising Strong*, "Sewer Rats & Scofflaws," (Speil & Grau, Penguin Random House, 2015), 109

2. "separation of normally related mental processes, resulting in one group functioning independently from the rest, leading in extreme cases to disorders such as multiple personality": *Lexico, s.v.*, "Dissociation," October 2019, https://www.lexico.com/en/definition/dissociation

3. Brene Brown, PHD, LMSW *Daring Greatly*, "Understanding & Combatting Shame," (Avery, an imprint of Penguin Random House 2012), 69

4. Brown, *Daring Greatly*, 26

5. Brown, *Daring Greatly*, 27

6. "Missing and Murdered Indigenous Women," Seeding Sovereignty, accessed October 2019, https://seedingsovereignty.org/mmiw

7. Roeder, Amy, "America is Faliling Its Black Mothers," Harvard Public Health, accessed Ocotober 2019, https://www.hsph.harvard.edu/magazine/magazine_article/america-is-failing-its-black-mothers/

8. "Survey finds disordered eating behaviors among three out of four American Women," UNC School of Medicine, accessed October 2019, http://www.med.unc.edu/www/newsarchive/2008/april/survey-finds-disordered-eating-behaviors-among-three-out-of-four-american-women

9. *Lexico, s.v.,* "Patriarchy," October 2019, https://www.lexico.com/en/definition/patriarchy

10. Samaran, Nora, "The Opposite of Rape Culture is Burturance Culture," normasamaran.com, https://norasamaran.com/2016/02/11/the-opposite-of-rape-culture-is-nurturance-culture-2/comment-page-2/

11. Brown, *Rising Strong,* 179

12. Brown, *Rising Strong,* 180

13. *Lexico, s.v.,* "Privilege," October 2019, https://www.lexico.com/en/definition/privilege

14. Jo Saxton, *The Dream of You,* "Don't Call Me Pleasant," (Waterbrook publications, 2018), 21

15. *Lexico, s.v.,* "Practice," October 2019, https://www.lexico.com/en/definition/practice

Thank you for reading *Dear Sister: A Letter to the Sisterhood*.
If you enjoyed this book, please share an online review.

KEEP IN TOUCH WITH MEGAN WOODING

Website: meganwooding.com
Email: meganewooding@gmail.com
Facebook: https://www.facebook.com/meganewooding/
Instagram: @mwooding

Made in the USA
Lexington, KY
07 December 2019